CONTRACT LAW

Visit the *Law Express Series* Companion Website at **www.pearsoned.co.uk/lawexpress** to find valuable **student** learning material including:

■ A study plan test to assess how well you know the subject before you begin your revision, now broken down into targeted study units

■ Interactive quizzes with a variety of question types to test your knowledge of the main points from each chapter of the book

■ Further examination questions and guidelines for answering them

■ Interactive flashcards to help you revise the main terms and cases

■ Printable versions of the topic maps and checklists

Plus:

■ 'You be the marker' allows you to see exam questions and answers from the perspective of the examiner and includes notes on how an answer might be marked

■ Podcasts provide point-by-point instruction on how to answer a common exam question

The essential reference for all students of law

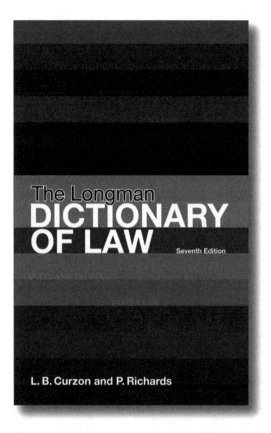

- Fully comprehensive entries on all aspects of English Law
- Clear definitions of specialised legal terminology
- Cross-referenced, giving full references for cases and statutes

The dictionary is fully supported by a companion website which links to additional legal information and provides updates to definitions.

Available from all good bookshops or order online at:
www.pearsoned.co.uk/law

CONTRACT LAW

Stefan Fafinski and Emily Finch

PEARSON

Longman

Harlow, England • London • New York • Boston • San Francisco • Toronto • Sydney • Singapore • Hong Kong
Tokyo • Seoul • Taipei • New Delhi • Cape Town • Madrid • Mexico City • Amsterdam • Munich • Paris • Milan

Pearson Education Limited
Edinburgh Gate
Harlow
Essex CM20 2JE
England

and Associated Companies throughout the world

Visit us on the World Wide Web at:
www.pearsoned.co.uk

First published 2008
Revised edition published 2009

© Pearson Education Limited 2008, 2009

ISBN: 978-1-4082-0433-7

British Library Cataloguing-in-Publication Data
A catalogue record for this book is available from the British Library

Library of Congress Cataloging-in-Publication Data
A catalog record for this book is available from the Library of Congress

10 9 8 7 6 5 4 3 2 1
12 11 10 09 08

Typeset by 3 in 10pt Helvetica Condensed
Printed and bound in Great Britain by Henry Ling Ltd, Dorchester, Dorset

The publisher's policy is to use paper manufactured from sustainable forests.

Contents

Supporting resources

Visit the *Law Express Series* Companion Website at **www.pearsoned.co.uk/lawexpress** to find valuable student learning material.

Companion Website for students

■ A study plan test to assess how well you know the subject before you begin your revision, now broken down into targeted study units
■ Interactive quizzes with a variety of question types to test your knowledge of the main points from each chapter of the book
■ Further examination questions and guidelines for answering them
■ Interactive flashcards to help you revise the main terms and cases
■ Printable versions of the topic maps and checklists
■ 'You be the marker' allows you to see exam questions and answers from the perspective of the examiner and includes notes on how an answer might be marked
■ Podcasts provide point-by-point instruction on how to answer a common exam question

Also: The Companion Website provides the following features:

■ Search tool to help locate specific items of content
■ E-mail results and profile tools to send results of quizzes to instructors
■ Online help and support to assist with website usage and troubleshooting

For more information please contact your local Pearson Education sales representative or visit **www.pearsoned.co.uk/lawexpress**

Acknowledgements

The authors would, as always, like to acknowledge the contributions of everyone who has reviewed drafts of this book for their comments and those who have provided general feedback on our other titles in the *Law Express* series. In particular we must once again single out Becky Taylor at Pearson Education for her unending patience and support during this latest project and Emma Easy for the thorough and professional manner in which she managed the production process.

We would also like to thank Elizabeth, just for being there; Johnno, because we can; and Chris, Tricia, Rebecca and Tom at the Dog and Duck, Emmbrook, for providing essential nutrition, good wine and friendship when we were exhausted from writing and the fridge was empty (as usual).

Finally, SF would like to thank his mother, as he hasn't done so in any of his other books and it's probably about time he did.

Stefan Fafinski
Emily Finch
October 2007

■Publisher's acknowledgements

Our thanks go to all reviewers who contributed to the development of this text, including students who participated in research and focus groups which helped to shape the series format.

Introduction

Contract law is one of the core subjects required for a qualifying law degree so it is a compulsory component of most undergraduate law programmes. It is usually taught as a first or second year subject as many of its concepts are relatively straightforward.

This revision guide will help you to identify the relevant law and apply it to factual situations which should help to overcome preconceived notions of the 'right' outcome in favour of legally accurate assessments of the liability of the parties. The book also provides guidance on the policy underlying the law and it identifies problem areas, both of which will help you to prepare for essay questions. The book is intended to supplement your course materials, lectures and textbooks; it is a guide to revision rather than a substitute for the amount of reading (and thinking) that you need to do in order to succeed. Contract law is a vast subject – you should realise this from looking at the size of your recommended textbook – so it follows that a revision guide cannot cover all the depth and detail that you need to know and it does not set out to do so. Instead, it aims to provide a concise overall picture of the key areas for revision – reminding you of the headline points to enable you to focus your revision, identify the key principles of law and use these effectively in essays and problem questions.

REVISION NOTES

Things to bear in mind when revising contract law:

- Do use this book to guide you through the revision process.
- Do not use this book to tell you everything that you need to know about contract law but make frequent reference to your recommended textbook and notes that you have made yourself from lectures and private study.
- Make sure that you consult your syllabus frequently to check which topics are covered and in how much detail.
- Read around the subject as much as possible to ensure that you have sufficient depth of knowledge. Use the suggested reading in this book and on your lecture handouts to help you to select relevant material.
- Take every possible opportunity to practise your essay-writing and problem-solving technique; get as much feedback as you can.

■ You should aim to revise as much of the syllabus as possible. Be aware that in contract law many questions that you encounter in coursework and examination papers could combine different topics, e.g. contract formation, misrepresentation and mistake. Therefore, selective revision could leave you unable to answer questions that include reference to material that you have excluded from your revision; it is never a good idea to tackle a question if you are able to deal with only part of the law that is raised.

Guided tour

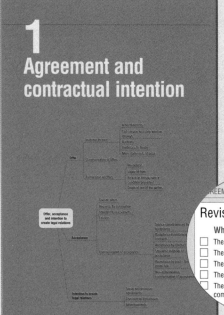

Topic maps – Highlight the main points and allow you to find your way quickly and easily through each chapter.

Revision checklist – How well do you know each topic? Don't panic if you don't know them all, the chapters will help you revise each point so that you will be fully prepared for your exams.

Sample questions – Prepare for what you will be faced with in your exams! Guidance on structuring strong answers is provided at the end of the chapter.

Sample question

Could you answer this question? Below is a typical problem question that could arise on this topic. Guidelines on answering the question are included at the end of the chapter, whilst a sample essay question and guidance on tackling it can be found on the Companion Website.

Problem question

On Wednesday, Tom, a vintage car dealer, placed an advertisement in a weekly motor sports magazine offering to sell a Triumph TR6 for £10,000, cheque accepted. Chris saw the advertisement on Thursday and immediately posted a letter to Tom saying

Key definition boxes – Make sure you understand essential legal terms.

KEY DEFINITION

The principle that a valid acceptance must correspond exactly with the terms of the offer is sometimes referred to as the **mirror image rule**.

Problem area boxes – Highlight areas where students most often trip up in exams. Use them to make sure you do not make the same mistakes.

> **Problem area:** The postal rule
>
> You must remember that the postal rule (if it applies at all) *applies to acceptances only, and not to the revocation of an offer by post.* It is a very common error to state that an offer was revoked by letter at the time that the letter was posted because of the postal rule. Be careful to avoid falling into this trap.

Key case and key statute boxes – Identify the essential cases and statutes that you need to know for your exams.

> ance occurs at the
>
> **KEY CASE**
>
> **British Car Auctions** v. **Wrig**
>
> Concerning: auctions; invitatio
>
> Facts
> The defendants were prosecuted fo
> The prosecution failed.
>
> Legal principle
> The car had not been offered t
> treat (bid).

> **KEY STATUTE**
>
> **Sale of Goods Act 1979, section 57(2)**
>
> 'A sale by auction is complete when the auctioneer a
> by the fall of the hammer, or in other customary mar
> announcement is made any bidder may retract his bi

Further thinking boxes – Illustrate areas of academic debate, and point you towards that extra reading required for the top grades.

> **FURTHER THINKING**
>
> Consideration is straightforward when the value is pecuniary, i.e. can be expressed in terms of a sum of money, but this is not the only way in which something can be viewed as valuable. For example, in *White* v. *Bluett* (1853) a son attempted to claim that he did not owe his late father's estate repayment of a sum of money due on a promissory note since he had agreed with his father that the debt would be written off in return for his promise not to complain about his father's will. This promise not to complain was held to be insufficiently tangible to amount to good consideration. However, in *Ward* v. *Byham* (1956) a mother's promise to keep her illegitimate child 'well looked after and happy' in return for money towards the child's upkeep from its father was held to be sufficient

Glossary – Forgotten the meaning of a word? Where a word is highlighted in the text, turn to the glossary at the back of the book to remind yourself of its meaning.

Glossary of terms

The glossary is divided into two parts: **key definitions** and **other useful terms**. The key definitions can be found within the chapters in which they occur as well as at the end of the book. These definitions are the essential terms that you must know and understand in order to prepare for an exam. The additional list of terms provides further definitions of useful terms and phrases which will also help you answer examination and coursework questions effectively. These terms are highlighted in the text as they occur but the definition can only be found here.

Key definitions

Term	Definition
Acceptance	Final and unqualified expression of assent to the terms of an offer.
Actionable misrepresentation	A statement of material fact made prior to the contract by one party to the contract to the other which is false or misleading and which induced the

Exam tips – Want to impress examiners? These indicate how you can improve your exam performance and your chances of getting top marks.

> **EXAM TIP**
>
> If a problem question involves a situation where one party to a contractual agreement is desperate (for whatever reason) for the other party to complete their promise on time then this is a good clue that a discussion of *Williams* v. *Roffey* will be required.

Revision notes – Highlight points that you should be aware of in other topic areas, or where your course may adopt a specific approach that you should check with your course tutor before reading further.

> **REVISION NOTE**
>
> This section covers only the very basic details of land law sufficient to illustrate the points relating to privity of contract. If you have already studied land law, it might be useful to look back at your materials on restrictive covenants and leases to refresh your memory on the principles before proceeding to cover the rest of this section.

Guided tour of the companion website

 Book resources are available to download. Print your own **topic maps** and **revision checklists!**

 Use the **study plan** prior to your revision to help you assess how well you know the subject and determine which areas need most attention. Choose to take the full assessment or focus on targeted study units.

 'Test your knowledge' of individual areas with quizzes tailored specifically to each chapter. A variety of multiple choice, true and false and fill-in-the-blank question types ensure you are prepared for anything. Sample problem and essay questions are also available with guidance on crafting a good answer.

 Flashcards help improve recall of important legal terms and key cases. Use online, print for a handy reference or download to iPod for on-the-go revision!

'**You be the marker**' gives you the chance to evaluate sample exam answers for different question types and understand how and why an examiner awards marks.

Download the **podcast** and listen as your own personal Law Express tutor guides you through a 10-15 minute audio session. You will be presented with a typical but challenging question and provided a step-by-step explanation on how to approach the question, what essential elements your answer will need for a pass, how to structure a good response, and what to do to make your answer stand out so that you can earn extra marks.

All of this and more can be found when you visit **www.pearsoned.co.uk/lawexpress**

Table of cases and statutes

■ Cases

Statutory instruments

European legislation

1
Agreement and contractual intention

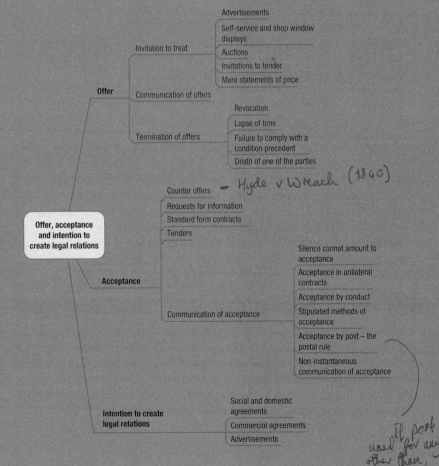

- Offer
  - Invitation to treat
    - Advertisements
    - Self-service and shop window displays
    - Auctions
    - Invitations to tender
    - Mere statements of price
  - Communication of offers
  - Termination of offers
    - Revocation
    - Lapse of time
    - Failure to comply with a condition precedent
    - Death of one of the parties

Offer, acceptance and intention to create legal relations

- Acceptance
  - Counter offers — *Hyde v Wrench (1840)*
  - Requests for information
  - Standard form contracts
  - Tenders
  - Communication of acceptance
    - Silence cannot amount to acceptance
    - Acceptance in unilateral contracts
    - Acceptance by conduct
    - Stipulated methods of acceptance
    - Acceptance by post – the postal rule
    - Non-instantaneous communication of acceptance

- Intention to create legal relations
  - Social and domestic agreements
  - Commercial agreements
  - Advertisements

If post used for anything other than acceptance, must be received

A printable version of this topic map is available from www.pearsoned.co.uk/lawexpress

Revision Checklist

an expression of willingness to contract on specified terms which when accepted will be binding

What you need to know:

- [ ] The definitions of offer and acceptance — *the unqualified assent to the terms of an offer which is legally binding*
- [ ] The distinction between an offer, an invitation to treat and a counter offer
- [ ] The rules on communication and withdrawal of offers
- [ ] The rules relating to communication of acceptances
- [ ] The presumptions of legal intent which arise in social, domestic and commercial situations.

Introduction:
Offer, acceptance and intention to create legal relations

Offer, acceptance and intention to create legal relations are three of the essential elements in the formation of a valid contract.

This chapter will deal with three of the four composite parts of a binding contract. The final part, consideration, will be covered in Chapter 2. Since a contract is an agreement, it follows that, in order for such an agreement to be reached, there must be an offer made by one party which is accepted by the other. Moreover, to distinguish simple informal agreements from those which are enforced or recognised by law, the parties to the contract must intend to create legal relations between each other.

Essay question advice

Essays on contract formation are uncommon. However, if an essay question does arise it is likely to cover one specific area of the topic in detail – for instance, whether the postal rule has any place in modern times. These sorts of question require an in-depth focus on specific parts of the material. Since offer, acceptance and intention to create legal relations cover an immense amount of material, essays that consider it as a whole are unlikely.

Problem question advice

Problem questions on contract formation are very common. They tend to involve a complex set of facts in which various parties communicate various things to each other by various means and at various times. It is often quite daunting to be faced with a lengthy scenario. However, if you are systematic in your approach, breaking down the facts into a sequence of events and dealing with each issue that comes up in turn, then you should end up with a well-structured argument that should be easier for the marker to follow. Since the vast majority of this topic is governed by case law it is important to remember to support every legal rule that you put forward in furtherance of your argument by an appropriate and relevant case authority.

Sample question

Could you answer this question? Below is a typical problem question that could arise on this topic. Guidelines on answering the question are included at the end of the chapter, whilst a sample essay question and guidance on tackling it can be found on the Companion Website.

Problem question

On Wednesday, Tom, a vintage car dealer, placed an advertisement in a weekly motor sports magazine offering to sell a Triumph TR6 for £10,000, cheque accepted. Chris saw the advertisement on Thursday and immediately posted a letter to Tom saying that he would be willing to pay £8,000 cash and giving his office fax number. On Friday morning, Tom replied by fax: 'Cheque preferred for advertised amount. Yours for that unless I hear from you to the contrary'. On receipt of the fax Chris posted a cheque for £10,000. However, at 6.45 pm on Friday evening Tom decided not to sell the car to Chris and sent a fax to him at his office to tell him so. The office had closed for the weekend when the fax arrived. Chris did not see it until early Monday morning. Chris's letter arrived at Tom's address on Saturday but was not opened by him until late Monday morning. On Saturday, Tom sold the car to Sam for £8,000 in cash. Chris now claims that Tom is in breach of contract.

Advise Chris of his legal position.

Offer

KEY DEFINITIONS

An **offer** is an expression of willingness to contract on specified terms, made with the intention that it is to become binding as soon as it is accepted by the person to whom it is addressed.

(Treitel, G.H. (2003) *The Law of Contract*, London: Sweet & Maxwell, page 8)

The party who makes an offer is known as the **offeror**.

The party to whom the offer is addressed is known as the **offeree**.

Originally the courts would determine whether or not an agreement had been reached between the parties by determining whether there had been a meeting of the minds. However, the courts now adopt an *objective* test as to the offeror's intention. Therefore if a reasonable person believed that the alleged offeror implied by his words or conduct that he intended to be bound then this may be sufficient for the offer actually to be valid in law, regardless of his actual state of mind. Examples of this include:

▮ A university which made an unconditional offer of a place to an applicant in error (*Moran* v. *University College Salford (No. 2)* (1994))
▮ A solicitor who mistakenly offered to settle a claim for £150,000 rather than the $155,000 which he had been instructed to offer by his client (*OT Africa Line Ltd* v. *Vickers plc* (1996)).

An important distinction must be made between an offer and an **invitation to treat**.

Invitation to treat

KEY DEFINITION

An **invitation to treat** is a preliminary statement expressing a willingness to receive offers.

An invitation to treat is therefore a statement made by a party inviting offers which that party is then free to accept or reject. An invitation to treat always precedes any offer. This can be illustrated as shown. Figure 1.1 demonstrates the steps in the formation of a simple contract.

Where there is an invitation to treat, this will precede the offer and reverse the parties who make the offer and acceptance (see Figure 1.2).

Figure 1.1

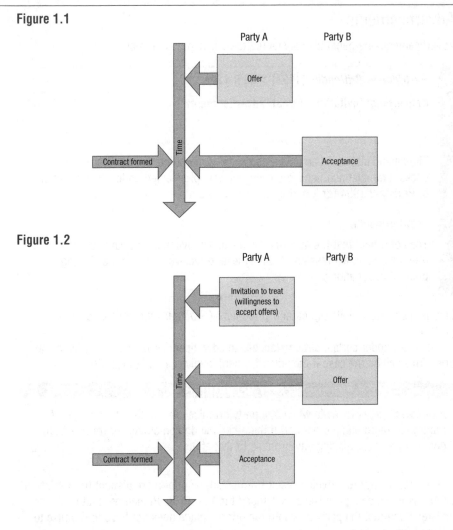

Figure 1.2

Although it might seem difficult to distinguish between a genuine offer and a mere invitation to treat since this will depend on the intention of the party making the statement, there are certain situations in which the distinction can be made by applying rules of law. These include:

∎ advertisements
∎ self-service and shop window displays
∎ auctions
∎ invitations to tender
∎ mere statements of price.

Advertisements

Advertisements are generally considered to be invitations to treat.

Partridge v. Crittenden [1968] 1 WLR 1204

Concerning: invitation to treat; advertisements

Facts
The defendant placed an advertisement in a magazine stating 'Bramblefinch cocks, bramblefinch hens 25s each'. He was prosecuted under the Protection of Birds Act 1954 for 'offering for sale' wild birds.

Legal principle
The court held that the advertisement was an invitation to treat and not an offer. It was an expression of willingness to receive offers as the starting point of negotiations.

This is also true of catalogues and price lists (*Grainger and Sons* v. *Gough* (1896)).

However, under certain circumstances, an advertisement *may* be regarded as an offer. This will be the case if the advertisement involves a **unilateral offer**.

KEY DEFINITION

A **unilateral offer** is made when one party promises to pay the other a sum of money (or to do some other act) if the other will do something (or forbear from doing so) without making any promise to that effect.

Unilateral contracts (which result from unilateral offers) are distinct from **bilateral contracts** in which a promise is exchanged for a promise. Remember that in a unilateral contract the party to whom the offer is made does not have to promise to do anything in return:

Bilateral contract	Unilateral contract
A promise in return for a promise	A promise in return for an act
Offer and acceptance are both promises	An 'if…' contract – offer is a promise
Both parties are immediately bound (provided there is consideration and intention to create legal relations)	Offeror is bound only if the specific act is performed (provided there is consideration and intention to create legal relations)

Therefore, if an advertisement indicates that the advertiser promises to pay something in return for a particular course of action then the advertiser is bound by that promise. For instance, an advertisement that states '£100 will be paid to anyone who can find my dog, Lassie is a unilateral offer; however, saying to someone 'I will give you £100 if you find my dog, Lassie is a bilateral offer. It is the promise that is important here: the fact that it is made in the form of an advertisement (which would normally be regarded as an invitation to treat) is irrelevant.

KEY CASE

Carlill v. *Carbolic Smoke Ball Company Ltd* [1893] 1 QB 256

Concerning: unilateral offer; advertisements

Facts

The defendants sold a patent medicine (the 'smoke ball'). They placed a newspaper advertisement stating that they would pay £100 (a very large sum of money in 1893) to anyone who 'contracts the increasing epidemic influenza, colds, or any disease caused by taking cold, after having used the ball three times daily for two weeks according to the printed directions supplied with each ball'. The claimant caught flu after using the ball as directed and claimed the sum of £100. The defendants claimed that the advertisement was a 'mere puff' and that, in any case, there was no offer made to any particular person and it was impossible to contract with the whole world.

Legal principle

The Court of Appeal held that the offer in the advertisement was a unilateral offer to the world at large which was accepted by the claimant. This unilateral offer waived the need for communication of acceptance prior to a claim being made on the basis of it. The claimant was therefore entitled to the £100.

The principle from *Carlill* also applies to advertisements offering rewards. These are traditionally treated as offers, rather than as invitations to treat, since there is an intention for the offeror to be bound as soon as the information is given (*Williams* v. *Carwardine* (1833)).

Self-service and shop window displays

When goods are on display in a self-service shop or in a shop window, their display does not constitute an offer: it is an invitation to treat.

KEY CASE

Pharmaceutical Society of Great Britain v. *Boots Cash Chemists Ltd* [1953] 1 All ER 482

Concerning: display of goods in a self-service shop; invitation to treat

Facts

The defendants changed the format of their shop from counter service to self service. Section 18 of the Pharmacy and Poisons Act 1933 provided that the sale of certain drugs should not occur 'other than under the supervision of a registered pharmacist'.

Legal principle

The Court of Appeal considered whether the contract was formed at the time that the customer removed the goods from the shelves (not under the supervision of a registered pharmacist) or at the time that the goods were presented at the counter for payment (under the supervision of a registered pharmacist). It was held that the contract was formed when the goods were presented at the cash desk and that the display of goods on the shelf was merely an invitation to treat.

This means that the offer to purchase is made at the cash desk by the purchaser. The shop is then free to accept this offer or reject it. This means that shops are not compelled to sell goods at the price at which they are displayed as the purchaser is offering to buy the item at the stated price at the checkout: the shopkeeper can reject that offer if desired.

The principle from *Boots Cash Chemists* was also applied in a case involving the display of goods in a shop window.

KEY CASE

Fisher v. *Bell* [1961] 1 QB 394

Concerning: display of goods in a self-service shop; invitation to treat

Facts

A shopkeeper displayed a flick knife in his window. The Offensive Weapons Act 1959 prohibited the 'offering for sale' of various offensive weapons, including flick knives. The shopkeeper was prosecuted under the Act.

▶

KEY CASE

Legal principle

The prosecution failed. The court held that the display of the knife in the window was an invitation to treat rather than an offer. Therefore the shopkeeper was not offering it for sale.

Auctions

In a sale at auction, the lot itself (together with the auctioneer's request for bids) is an invitation to treat. Each bid represents an offer to buy the lot at the price offered. Acceptance occurs at the fall of the auctioneer's hammer.

KEY CASE

British Car Auctions v. Wright [1972] 1 WLR 1519

Concerning: auctions; invitation to treat

Facts

The defendants were prosecuted for offering an unroadworthy vehicle for sale. The prosecution failed.

Legal principle

The car had not been offered for sale; there had only been an invitation to treat (bid).

This position is also upheld by section 57(2) of the Sale of Goods Act 1979:

KEY STATUTE

Sale of Goods Act 1979, section 57(2)

'A sale by auction is complete when the auctioneer announces its completion by the fall of the hammer, or in other customary manner; and until the announcement is made any bidder may retract his bid'.

However, where there is an auction sale 'without reserve' (i.e. there is no minimum price that must be reached before the offer is accepted) then this equates to an offer to sell to the highest bidder which is accepted by the submission of the highest bid. This principle was first stated *obiter* in *Harris* v. *Nickerson* (1873) and was followed by the Court of Appeal in *Barry* v. *Davies (t/a Heathcote Ball (Commercial Auctions) & Co)* (2000).

Invitations to tender

Invitations to tender are normally invitations to treat: therefore the person making the invitation to tender is not bound to accept any of the responses (offers) to the tender (*Spencer* v. *Harding* (1870)).

However, if the person making the tender states that he will accept the highest offer to buy goods or the lowest offer for the supply of goods or services, then the tender may be considered to be either an offer or an invitation to submit offers with the undertaking to accept the most favourable, concluding the contract at the time that the best offer is communicated (*Harvela Investments Ltd* v. *Royal Trust of Canada (CI) Ltd* (1986)).

Parties issuing invitations to tender are bound to consider (though not necessarily to accept) a tender properly submitted before any deadline (*Blackpool and Fylde Aero Club* v. *Blackpool Borough Council* (1990)).

Mere statements of price

Where a party simply states the minimum price at which they would be willing to sell, this is an invitation to treat rather than an offer.

KEY CASE

Harvey v. *Facey* [1893] AC 552

Concerning: statements of price; invitation to treat

Facts

Facey was going to sell his store to Kingston when Harvey and another telegraphed him a message stating 'Will you sell us Bumper Hall Pen? Telegraph lowest cash price—answer paid.'

Facey answered by telegram, 'Lowest price for Bumper Hall Pen £900.'

Harvey answered by telegram, 'We agree to buy Bumper Hall Pen for the sum of nine hundred pounds asked by you.'

Harvey claimed that he had accepted the offer and sued for specific performance of the agreement, and for an injunction to restrain Kingston from taking a conveyance of the property.

Legal principle

There had been no offer. Facey's statement was merely a statement of price and not an offer capable of acceptance.

In a similar case, a local authority wrote to a tenant stating that it may 'be prepared to sell' his council house to him at a stated price together with an application form. The tenant completed the form and returned it to the council. However, a change in council policy meant that the sale did not proceed. The tenant's claim for breach of contract failed, since his completed application form was held to be an offer to buy in response to the council's initial letter which was an invitation to treat (*Gibson* v. *Manchester City Council* (1979)). It is worth noting, however, that the form of words used can render it sufficiently precise to be an offer capable of acceptance. In *Storer* v. *Manchester City Council* (1974), a case which also involved the sale of a council house, the tenant returned a form headed 'Agreement for Sale'. In this case, the court held that the form had a specific character that made it an offer rather than an invitation to treat, which the tenant had accepted by signing and returning it.

Communication of offers

In order to be valid an offer must be communicated to the offeree. This means that no party can be bound by an offer of which they were unaware (*Taylor* v. *Laird* (1856)). This is true for unilateral as well as bilateral offers: therefore, the offeree must have clear knowledge of the existence of the offer for it to be valid (and thus enforceable) (*Inland Revenue Commissioners* v. *Fry* (2001)). You have already seen that unilateral offers can be made to the whole world and may be accepted (by performing the conditions named in it) by anyone who had notice of the offer (*Carlill* v. *Carbolic Smoke Ball Co.* (1893)).

Termination of offers

Offers may cease to exist in a number of ways. Acceptance and express rejection are straightforward situations. If an offer is accepted then a contract is formed (provided that the other elements of the contract – intention to create legal relations and consideration – are present). The offer may simply be refused (in which case there is no contract) or extinguished by a counter offer (see 'Acceptance' later in this chapter). In addition, offers may be terminated by:

■ revocation
■ lapse of time
■ failure to comply with a condition precedent
■ death of one of the parties.

Revocation

KEY DEFINITION

Revocation refers to the rescinding, annulling or withdrawal of an offer.

Generally speaking an offer may be withdrawn at any time *prior to acceptance* (*Routledge* v. *Grant* (1828)). The revocation must also be *communicated* to the offeree:

KEY CASE

Bryne v. *Van Tienhoven* (1880) 5 CPD 344

Concerning: communication of revocation

Facts

On 1 October, a letter offering to sell tinplates was posted from Van Tienhoven in Cardiff to Byrne in New York.

On 8 October, the offerors changed their minds and posted a letter of revocation withdrawing the offer made by letter on 1 October.

On 11 October, Byrne received the letter offering to sell (from 1 October) and accepted by telegram.

On 15 October, Byrne confirmed the acceptance (from 11 October) by letter.

On 20 October, Byrne received the letter of 8 October withdrawing the offer.

Legal principle

The offer of 1 October had not been withdrawn at the time that it was accepted and therefore the contract was formed on acceptance on 11 October. This was so despite the lack of agreement between the parties.

EXAM TIP

Exam questions involving offer and acceptance often involve the communcation of revocation between the parties. Remember that an offer is valid until it is revoked and that the revocation must be communicated to the offeree. It is often useful when faced with a question involving facts relating to contract formation to draw a timeline as to 'what happened when' and then to analyse each stage in turn. An example of such a timeline will be provided later in this chapter once we have considered acceptance.

Although any revocation of an offer must be communicated, it does not always have to be communicated by the offeror themselves. Revocation made by a third party is valid provided that:

∎ the third party is a reliable source of information; and
∎ the third party is one on whom both parties can rely (*Dickinson* v. *Dodds* (1876)).

The situation is different with regard to unilateral offers. Since a unilateral offer is a promise in return for an act, it may be accepted by anyone who performs the act stipulated in the offer. Therefore, in order to revoke a unilateral offer (to the world at large) the offeror must take reasonable steps to notify those persons who might be likely to accept. *Shuey* v. *United States* (1875) is generally accepted authority for this proposition, although it is an American case and therefore carries only persuasive authority in England and Wales.

If the offeree has started performance of the act specified in a unilateral offer then it may not be revoked, even if the act is incomplete.

KEY CASE

Errington v. *Errington & Woods* [1952] 1 KB 290

Concerning: revocation of a unilateral offer

Facts

A father bought a house with a mortgage for his son and daughter-in-law to live in. He promised that he would transfer legal title to the property to them if they paid off all the mortgage repayments. The couple did not make any promise in return. The father died after some repayments had been made. Other family members claimed possession of the house, title to which remained in the name of the father. Their claim failed.

Legal principle

The contract was a unilateral contract, since it involved an act (payment of the mortgage) in return for a promise (to transfer the house once all the payments had been made). Once performance had commenced (by the mortgage repayments being made) then the father's promise could not be revoked. However, Lord Denning also stated that the promise would not be binding if the act was left incomplete and unperformed. Therefore, as long as the couple continued to make all the mortgage payments until it was fully paid off then the father's promise to transfer the house to them would still be binding.

The principle from *Errington* v. *Errington & Woods* was also accepted by the Court of Appeal *obiter* in the later case of *Daulia Ltd* v. *Four Millbank Nominees Ltd* (1978) where Goff LJ stated that:

'In unilateral contracts the offeror is entitled to require full performance of the condition imposed otherwise he is not bound. That must be subject to one important qualification – there must be an implied obligation on the part of the offeror not to prevent the condition being satisfied, an obligation which arises as soon as the offeree starts to perform. Until then the offeror can revoke the whole thing, but once the offeree has embarked on performance, it is too late for the offeror to revoke his offer.'

Lapse of time

An offer may not stay open for ever. An offer may state that it is to terminate on a particular date or after a certain fixed period, after which it is no longer capable of acceptance. Alternatively, where there is no particular date specified for the offer to terminate, then it will in any case lapse after a reasonable time has passed.

> **KEY CASE**
>
> ### *Ramsgate Victoria Hotel Co. Ltd* v. *Montefiore* (1866) LR 1 Ex 109
>
> **Concerning: lapse of offer; reasonable time**
>
> **Facts**
>
> The claimant had offered to buy shares in the hotel company in June, but the company did not issue the shares for sale until November.
>
> **Legal principle**
>
> The court held that an offer would lapse after a 'reasonable time'. What is reasonable would depend on the offer and the subject matter of the contract. In cases where the value of the subject matter of the contract could fluctuate rapidly (like the shares in this particular case) or where the subject matter was perishable, then the offer would terminate after a short time.

This principle is also true of offers made by telegram (*Quenerduaine* v. *Cole* (1883)) or similar expedient means of communication such as telex (a system of telegraphy in which printed messages are transmitted and received by teleprinters using the public telecommunication lines) or fax.

Failure to comply with a condition precedent

An offer may also terminate if the parties to it had agreed to meet certain conditions and then failed to do so. For instance, an offer to sell a car on hire-purchase was considered to be subject to the condition that it would remain in the same condition from the time of the offer to the time of acceptance. Therefore, when the car in question had been damaged due to its being stolen from the showroom before the contract was concluded the offer was rendered incapable of being accepted (*Financings Ltd* v. *Stimson* (1962)). The same situation applies where job offers are made subject to satisfactory references, Criminal Records Bureau checks or medical reports.

Death of one of the parties

Death of the offeror

Where the offeror dies before the offer is accepted, then the offeror's personal representatives may still be bound by an acceptance provided that:

■ the contract does not involve the personal services of the deceased, and
■ the offeree is ignorant of the offeror's death (*Bradbury* v. *Morgan* (1862)).

Death of the offeree

Where the offeree dies before acceptance, then the offer lapses and the offeree's personal representatives will be unable to accept on behalf of the deceased (*Reynolds* v. *Atherton* (1921)).

■ Acceptance

KEY DEFINITION

An **acceptance** is a final and unqualified expression of assent to the terms of an offer.

(Treitel, G.H. (2003) *The Law of Contract*, London: Sweet & Maxwell, page 16)

Since acceptance is a final and unqualified assent to the terms of an offer, it must correspond exactly with the offer made. It must be unequivocal and unconditional.

KEY DEFINITION

The principle that a valid acceptance must correspond exactly with the terms of the offer is sometimes referred to as the **mirror image rule**.

Counter offers

Since an acceptance must correspond exactly with the terms of the offer in order for it to be valid, it follows that a response which introduces new terms or attempts to vary terms proposed in the offer is not valid. In this case the response becomes a *counter offer* which destroys the original offer, rendering it incapable of acceptance.

Hyde v. *Wrench* (1840) 49 ER 132

Concerning: acceptance; counter offer

Facts

Wrench offered to sell a farm to Hyde for £1,000. Hyde rejected this price and offered to pay £950. Wrench rejected Hyde's offer. Wrench then sold the farm to a third party. Hyde attempted to accept the original offered price of £1,000 and sue Wrench for breach of contract when Wrench sold the farm to another party.

Legal principle

Hyde's claim was rejected. The court held that the counter offer of £950 had impliedly rejected the original offer and, since the original offer had been destroyed, it was no longer open for Hyde to accept.

Lord Langdale stated that:

'If [the offer] had at once been unconditionally accepted, there would undoubtedly have been a perfect binding contract; instead of that, the plaintiff [now referred to as the claimant] made an offer of his own, to purchase the property for £950, and he thereby rejected the offer previously made by the defendant. I think that it was not afterwards competent for him to revive the proposal of the defendant, by tendering an acceptance of it; and that, therefore, there exists no obligation of any sort between the parties.'

Since a counter offer destroys the original offer, the roles of offeror and offeree become reversed. The party who made the original offer may accept the counter offer, reject the counter offer, or make a counter offer in return (in which case the roles reverse again). This can continue until agreement is finally reached as depicted in Figure 1.3.

Requests for information

A mere request for information is treated differently to a counter offer.

Stevenson, Jaques & Co. v. *McLean* (1880) 5 QBD 346

Concerning: acceptance; request for information

Facts

McLean telegraphed Stevenson offering to sell 3,800 tons of iron 'at 40 s net cash per ton, open till Monday'. On Monday morning Stevenson telegrammed

McLean: 'Please wire whether you would accept 40 for delivery over two months or if not longest limit you would give'. McLean did not respond and at 1.34 pm Stevenson telegrammed again, accepting the original offer. McLean had already sold the iron to a third party of which he advised Stevenson by telegram at 1.25 pm. That telegram crossed with Stevenson's second telegram. Stevenson sued for breach of contract.

Legal principle

Stevenson's first telegram was not a counter offer. It was a mere request for information. Consequently, McLean's offer was still open at 1.34 pm. It was validly accepted. Therefore there was a valid contract of which McLean was in breach. As Lush J said:

> 'Here there is no counter-proposal. The words are: 'Please wire whether you would accept forty for delivery over two months, or if not, the longest limit you would give.' There is nothing specific by way of offer or rejection, but a mere inquiry, which should have been answered and not treated as a rejection of the offer.'

Therefore, if a response is made to an offer which does not attempt to vary the terms of the offer it is not a counter offer, since it does not reject the terms of the offer. It is therefore still open to acceptance by the offeree.

Figure 1.3

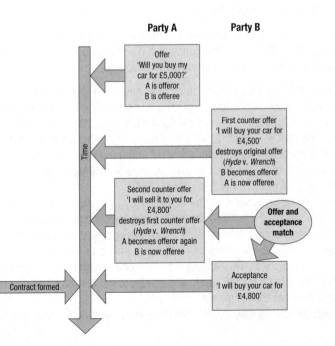

Once you have identified an offer in the facts of a problem question, look out for any communications from the offeree and analyse these to determine whether they amount to a request for information (which allows the original offer to stand) or whether they amount to a counter-offer (which destroys the original offer and takes its place). A key distinction here is whether the offeree is asking for more detail (request for information) or whether he is suggesting an alternative set of terms (a counter-offer).

Standard form contracts

Problems can arise where one or both parties uses pre-prepared contract forms in relation to the general rule that the acceptance must correspond exactly to the offer.

The situation which arises where one or both parties attempts to rely on their standard terms is often referred to as the **battle of the forms**.

This situation may arise as follows:

▮ A makes an offer to B on a form containing A's standard terms of business
▮ B 'accepts' A's offer on a form containing B's standard terms of business
▮ A's standard terms and B's standard terms conflict.

At this stage, there is no contract, since offer and acceptance do not match. Generally speaking, in the case of conflict, each communication is considered to be a counter offer so that if a contract is formed (in such cases acceptance is usually inferred by conduct – see later in this chapter) then it must be on the terms of the last counter offer. This is deemed to have been accepted and it is the terms of the final counter offer which apply to the contract as a whole (see for example *Zambia Steel & Building Supplies Ltd* v. *James Clark & Eaton Ltd* (1986)).

In *British Road Services* v. *Arthur V. Crutchley Ltd* (1968) the claimants had delivered a quantity of whisky to the defendants for storage. The delivery driver handed the defendants a delivery note which incorporated the claimants' 'conditions of carriage'. This note was stamped by the defendants as 'Received under [the defendants'] conditions'. This was held to be a counter offer which the claimants had accepted by handing over the goods and therefore the contract incorporated the defendants' and not the claimants' conditions.

Although the courts may decide that there is no valid agreement and halt performance of the contract, they are reluctant to do so once performance has started *(British Steel Corporation* v. *Cleveland Bridge and Engineering Co.* (1984)).

However, a somewhat radical (and thus unlikely to be followed) departure from the strict offer/counter-offer analysis was offered in *Butler Machine Tool Co. Ltd* v. *Ex-Cell-O Corporation (England) Ltd* (1979) by Lord Denning who looked beyond the strict wording of the forms when he stated that:

> 'The terms and conditions of both parties are to be construed together. If they can be reconciled so as to give harmonious result, all well and good. If the differences are irreconcilable, so that they are mutually contradictory, then the conflicting terms may have to be scrapped and replaced by a reasonable implication.'

Tenders

Since an invitation to tender is usually an invitation to treat, the submission of a tender is usually an offer. However, the 'acceptance' of a tender does not always result in a binding contract:

■ Where the tender is submitted for supplying specific goods or services on a specific date, acceptance results in a binding contract.
■ Where the tender is submitted for supplying a specific quantity of goods over a specified period of time, acceptance results in a binding contract.
■ Where the tender is submitted for indefinite subject matter such as 'such quantities as you may order' or 'as and when required' then 'acceptance' of that tender does not result in a binding contract at that time. Acceptance occurs when an order is placed (*Percival* v. *London County Council Asylum, etc Committee* (1918)). Once an order is placed then the party who submitted the tender (the offer) is bound (*Great Northern Railway* v. *Witham* (1873)).

Communication of acceptance

Generally speaking, an acceptance has no effect until it is communicated to the offeror. In *Entores* v. *Miles Far East Corporation* (1955) Lord Denning explained the principle as follows:

> 'Let me first consider a case where two people make a contract by word of mouth in the presence of one another. Suppose, for instance, that I shout an offer to a man across a river or a courtyard but I do not hear his reply because it is drowned by an aircraft flying overhead. There is no contract at that moment. If he wishes to make a contract, he must wait till the aircraft is gone and then shout back his acceptance so that I can hear what he says. Not until I have his answer am I bound.'

Silence cannot amount to acceptance

Since acceptance must be communicated, it follows that silence can never constitute acceptance.

KEY CASE

Felthouse v. Brindley (1863) 142 ER 1037

Concerning: acceptance; silence

Facts

An uncle and nephew were negotiating the sale of the nephew's horse. The uncle had stated that 'if I hear no more from you I shall consider the horse mine at £30 15/-'.

The nephew did not reply but asked an auctioneer to withdraw the horse from an auction. The auctioneer forgot the instruction and the horse was sold to another party. In order to claim against the auctioneer, the uncle needed to prove that there was a contract between him and his nephew for the sale of the horse.

Legal principle

The court held that there was no contract since the nephew had never communicated his intention to accept to his uncle 'or done anything to bind himself'.

This principle was also considered in *The Leonidas D* (1985) where Goff LJ commented that it was 'axiomatic that acceptance of an offer cannot be inferred from silence, save in the most exceptional circumstances'.

Acceptance in unilateral contracts

In a **unilateral contract**, the rule that acceptance must be communicated is waived:

▌ The offer can be accepted by fully performing the stipulated act or forbearance (*Daulia Ltd* v. *Four Millbank Nominees Ltd* (1978))
▌ There is *no need to communicate* acceptance to the offeror (*Carlill* v. *Carbolic Smoke Ball Company* (1893); *Bowerman* v. *Association of British Travel Agents* (1995)).
▌ The offer can be withdrawn before it is accepted: the offer being accepted only by *some* performance.

EXAM TIP

If you are dealing with a unilateral offer in a problem question, determine whether it has been accepted by asking yourself the following questions:

▶

- What conduct did the offeror specify was required?
- What did the offeree do and did this match what the offeror required?
- If the offeree has done only part of what the offeror wanted, did the offeror intervene to prevent the offeree completing performance?
- Did the offeror have a change of heart and withdraw the offer? Did this happen before or after the offeree had embarked on performance?

Acceptance by conduct

Acceptance may be inferred from conduct without it being expressly communicated.

KEY CASE

***Brogden v. Metropolitan Railway Co* (1877) 2 App Cas 666**

Concerning: acceptance by conduct

Facts

Brogden was a colliery owner in Wales who supplied the Metropolitan Railway Company. In November 1871 a representative of Brogden suggested that a contract should be entered into. A draft contract was prepared and sent to Brogden who filled in the arbitration clause by nominating an arbitrator, appended the word 'Approved' and returned it to the railway. The railway's agent did not acknowledge it. In December 1871 the railway placed an order on the terms of the document, which Brogden fulfilled. The parties traded on the terms of the document until December 1873, when Brogden refused to continue to supply on that basis. The railway brought an action against Brogden for breach of contract. Brogden claimed that since the railway had never acknowledged the altered draft, which was a counter offer, there was no contract.

Legal principle

The House of Lords accepted that the completion of the arbitrator's name technically rendered it a counter offer. However, since the parties to the contract had traded on the terms of the contract then they had accepted the counter offer as part of the agreement and Brogden could not therefore claim that there was no contract.

Stipulated methods of acceptance

Although acceptance can generally be in any form, as long as it is communicated to the offeree (other than in the case of a unilateral contract), where the offer stipulates a particular method of acceptance, such as 'by return of post', 'by fax' or 'by telegram', then if the offeree uses a different method there may not be a contract (*Eliason* v. *Henshaw* (1819)) if the offeror clearly states that *only the stipulated method of acceptance will be sufficient.*

If the offeree uses an equally expeditious method of acceptance to that stipulated, then that should be sufficient. In *Tinn* v. *Hoffmann* (1873) the offeree was instructed to reply to an offer 'by return of post' to which Honeyman J said: 'That does not mean exclusively a reply by letter or return of post, but you may reply by telegram or by verbal message or by any other means not later than a letter written by return of post.' This principle was also applied in *Manchester Diocesan Council for Education* v. *Commercial & General Investments Ltd* (1970) such that an acceptance which meets the offeror's objective in prescribing a method of acceptance (albeit not by the method prescribed) will remain valid.

Finally, if the offer does not state a method of acceptance, the required speed of acceptance can be deduced from the means by which the offer was sent: therefore, for example, if an offer is made by telegram, then it is implied that acceptance should be made by an equally speedy means. Therefore an acceptance by post would be ineffective (*Quenerduaine* v. *Cole* (1883)).

Acceptance by post – the postal rule

Acceptance by post is an exception to the general rule that acceptance must come to the attention of the offeror before it is valid.

KEY CASE

Adams v. *Lindsell* (1818) 1 B & Ald 681

Concerning: acceptance by post; the 'postal rule'

Facts

Lindsell made an offer by post to sell Adams some wool, asking for a reply 'in course of post'. The offer letter was sent on 2 September, but it did not arrive until 5 September, whereupon Adams posted a letter of acceptance at once. By the time the letter of acceptance had arrived (which was after some lengthy time), Lindsell, who had assumed that his offer had been rejected, had sold the wool to a third party. Adams claimed breach of contract.

Legal principle

The court held that the contract was made at the time the letter was posted.

Problem area: The postal rule

You must remember that the postal rule (if it applies at all) *applies to acceptances only, and not to the revocation of an offer by post.* It is a very common error to state that an offer was revoked by letter at the time that the letter was posted because of the postal rule. Be careful to avoid falling into this trap.

Therefore the general 'postal rule' is that acceptance by post takes effect upon posting rather than delivery. However, there are certain conditions which relate to its use. For the postal rule to apply:

- Acceptance by post must have been requested by the offeror or acceptance by post must be a normal, reasonable or anticipated means of acceptance (*Henthorn* v. *Fraser* (1892)).
- The letter of acceptance must be properly stamped and addressed (*Re London & Northern Bank, ex parte Jones* (1990)).
- The letter of acceptance must be posted – that is, in the control of the Post Office (or whatever the universal postal service is called from time to time: *Brinkibon* v. *Stahag Stahl* (1983)). In *Re London & Northern Bank, ex parte Jones* (1990) a letter of acceptance that had been handed to a postman who was authorised only to *deliver* (not collect) was held *not* to have been posted.
- The postal rule must not have been expressly excluded in the offer. In *Holwell Securities* v. *Hughes* (1974) it was held that an offer which required acceptance 'by notice in writing' meant that actual communication of acceptance must reach the offeror and as such the claimants could not rely on the postal rule to assert the existence of a contract.
- Use of the postal rule must not create 'manifest inconvenience or absurdity' (*Holwell Securities* v. *Hughes* (1974)).

EXAM TIP

The postal rule is often encountered in problem questions on contract formation. Although most students conclude that where a letter of acceptance has been posted then the postal rule applies, the vast majority of those often forget to discuss the conditions which apply to the postal rule. However, you should see from this section that there are several provisos to the use of the postal rule. You can improve your answer by a brief consideration of the conditions which apply to the postal rule. While these exceptions may not apply to your particular question, in considering them, and supporting those considerations with case authority, you will have demonstrated a far greater depth of understanding which should make your answer stand out.

The postal rule also applies:

- if the letter of acceptance is received after notice of revocation of the offer has been sent (*Henthorn* v. *Fraser* (1892)).
- if the letter of acceptance is *never* received by the offeror (*Household Fire Insurance Co.* v. *Grant* (1879)).

Non-instantaneous communication of acceptance

Since the postal rule was developed, advances in communications technology have led to a number of situations where its use is irrelevant. Virtually instantaneous communications methods, such as telephone conversations, are treated in the same way as face-to-face personal conversations and are, therefore, relatively unproblematic: acceptance takes place when and where the acceptance is received (*Entores* v. *Miles Far East Corporation* (1955)).

However, the situation is more difficult when answering machines are used. A message may be left which is not played back for some time. The same is true of telex, fax and e-mail: all systems (when working correctly) deliver messages virtually instantaneously, but those messages may not be read instantly if the receiving party is away from the receiving machine. The question then becomes one of if, when and where a contract is formed with such non-instantaneous methods.

KEY CASE

Brinkibon v. *Stahag Stahl* [1983] 2 AC 34

Concerning: acceptance by non-instantaneous communications

Facts

An acceptance was sent by telex out of office hours.

Legal principle

The House of Lords held that a telex message that was sent outside office hours should not be considered to be an instantaneous means of communication and therefore acceptance could only be effective when the office re-opened.

Lord Wilberforce summarised the situation in relation to modern communications methods by stating that:

> 'No universal rule can cover all such cases; they must be resolved by reference to the intention of the parties, by sound business practice and in some cases by a judgment where the risk should lie.'

∎ Intention to create legal relations

In order to prevent the courts being troubled by disputes concerning agreements which are not intended to be legally binding, the courts have sought to distinguish agreements that should be legally enforceable and those which should not.

These fall into a number of categories:

∎ social and domestic agreements — *Errington v Errington* *Unilateral Contract* *Father died — left property to daughter*

■ commercial agreements
■ advertisements.

Social and domestic agreements

There is a presumption that there is no intention to create legal relations in social or domestic agreements. This presumption may be rebutted.

Husbands and wives

Agreements between husband and wife are presumed not to create legal relations unless the agreement itself states that it does (*Balfour* v. *Balfour* (1919)). However, if the couple are not living together amicably at the time of the agreement then the agreement between them may be considered to be legally binding (*Merritt* v. *Merritt* (1970)).

Parents and children

Domestic agreements between parents and children are presumed not to create legal relations (*Jones* v. *Padavatton* (1969)).

Parties sharing a house

Where an agreement is made between parties who share a dwelling but are not related, then the court will consider all the circumstances of the agreement. They are more likely to find the intention to be legally bound where money has changed hands (*Simpkins* v. *Pays* (1955)).

Other social agreements

The courts are reluctant to find contractual intention in social agreements. For instance, in *Lens* v. *Devonshire Club* (1914) it was held that the winner of a competition held by a golf club could not sue for his prize since 'no one concerned with that competition ever intended that there should be any legal results flowing from the conditions posted and the acceptance by the competitor of those conditions'.

Commercial agreements

Just as there is a presumption that there is no intention to create legal relations in social or domestic agreements the converse is true in commercial agreements: it is presumed that there is an intention to create legal relations.

This presumption can generally only be rebutted by express provision in the contract. In *Rose & Frank Co.* v. *Crompton Bros Ltd* (1925) it was held that a commercial agreement between a British manufacturer and their appointed distributor in the USA which expressly stated that it was 'not subject to legal jurisdiction' in either country was sufficient to rebut the presumption that it was intended to be a contract.

This is so even if the agreement appears to be gratuitous in nature, such as those involving an *ex gratia* payment (*Edwards* v. *Skyways* (1969)).

However, it does not apply to so-called 'comfort letters' which are interpreted as a statement of fact rather than as a contractual promise (*Kleinwort Benson Ltd* v. *Malaysian Mining Corporation* (1989)). It also does not apply to agreements (such as the football pools) which are stated to be 'binding in honour only' (*Jones* v. *Vernons Pools* (1938)).

Esso v Commissioners for Custom & Excise

Advertisements

Sellers often make claims in advertisements which are generally treated as a 'mere puff' and as such do not generally create legal relations. However, more specific pledges, such as 'we are never knowingly undersold, so if we find a competitor within the area selling the same product that is part of our own standard offer at a lower price, our shelf price will be reduced to match', are likely to be binding. A statement will not be binding if the court considers that it was not seriously meant (*Weeks* v. *Tybald* (1605)).

Chapter Summary:
Putting it all together

TEST YOURSELF

- [ ] Can you tick all the points from the revision checklist at the beginning of this chapter?
- [ ] Take the **end-of-chapter quiz** on the Companion Website.
- [ ] Test your knowledge of the cases below with the **revision flashcards** on the website.
- [ ] Attempt the problem question from the beginning of the chapter using the guidelines below.
- [ ] Go to the Companion Website to try out other questions.

Answer guidelines

See the problem question at the start of the chapter.

Points to remember when answering this question:

■ This question is concerned with contract formation. It will depend on the exact timing of communication of revocation and acceptance.

■ Start by untangling the facts by constructing a timeline as shown in Figure 1.4 overleaf. Then analyse each event in turn in terms of offer, acceptance and revocation.

■ The advertisement is likely to be construed as an *invitation to treat* (*Partridge* v. *Crittenden*) – that is an expression of willingness to accept offers – rather than as a unilateral offer (*Carlill*).

■ Therefore, since an invitation to treat can only be followed by an offer, Chris's letter on Thursday is an *offer* to buy the car for £8,000 in cash.

■ This offer is effective upon receipt by Tom on Friday morning. The postal rule does not apply to offers, only acceptances (*Adams* v. *Lindsell*).

■ Tom's fax in return on Friday morning in which he states he will only sell for the 'advertised amount' and would prefer payment by cheque does not match the offer made by Chris. It is therefore a counter offer which destroys Chris's offer (*Hyde* v. *Wrench*).

■ Tom's statement of 'yours for that unless I hear from you to the contrary' has no effect since silence cannot constitute acceptance (*Felthouse* v. *Brindley*).

■ Upon receipt of the fax, Chris sends an acceptance with a cheque for £10,000 by post. This acceptance matches the terms of the offer precisely (cheque, £10,000).

■ Does the postal rule apply? (*Adams* v. *Lindsell*). If so, it does not matter that the acceptance letter was not opened until late Monday morning: indeed it would not matter if the letter never arrived (*Household Fire Insurance Co.* v. *Grant*). It would be effective on posting and the contract would have been formed at that point on Friday morning.

■ There is nothing to suggest that the letter was improperly addressed or posted and Tom did not specify any specific means of acceptance (*Holwell Securities* v. *Hughes*).

■ Tom could argue that the postal rule does not apply since a letter is not an appropriate means of response to a fax (*Quenerduaine* v. *Cole*; *Henthorn* v. *Fraser*).

■ On Friday evening Tom sent a fax of revocation. Since this was outside normal office hours, the message is deemed not to have been communicated at this time. In general, instantaneous communications take place when and where received and the postal rule does not apply (*Entores* v. *Miles Far East Corporation*). However, following *Brinkibon* v. *Stahag Stahl,* no universal rule exists and the courts can take into account the intention of the parties, sound business practices and an assessment of where the risk should lie. Tom's fax of revocation is therefore likely to be deemed as communicated on Monday morning when Chris's office re-opens for business.

■ If the postal rule applies then Chris will have a contract for the car. Tom will also have a contract with Josh for the car. Tom will be in breach of one of these contracts.

■ Remedies which may be available to Chris will be discussed further in Chapter 9.

Figure 1.4

Tom — Places advertisement in magazine TR6 for sale £10,000, cheque accepted (Wednesday)

Chris — Posts letter to Tom Willing to pay £68,000 cash Office fax number (Thursday)

Tom — Replies by fax 'Cheque preferred for advertised amount. Yours for that unless I hear otherwise' (Friday am)

Chris — Posted letter with cheque for £10,000 (Friday am)

Tom — Sends fax revoking offer (Friday 6.45 pm)

Tom — Letter with cheque arrives (Saturday am)

Tom — Sells car to Josh for £8,000 cash (Saturday pm)

Chris — Sees fax of revocation (Monday early am)

Tom — Opens letter containing cheque (Monday late am)

Make your answer really stand out:

■ Although the question is concerned primarily with offer and acceptance, remember that these are only two of the essential elements of a contract. Although intention to create legal relations and consideration are unproblematic in this instance, a thorough answer will consider them both briefly. Since this is a commercial arrangement (Tom is a vintage car dealer) then the presumption that there is intention to create legal relations arises (there is nothing to suggest that it has been rebutted: *Rose & Frank Co.* v. *Crompton Bros Ltd*). Consideration will be satisfied by the price paid for the car (see Chapter 2).

▌In a question like this it is important to adopt a methodical approach to avoid a confused or rambling answer that is difficult for the marker to follow. If you are not expressing your line of argument with sufficient clarity you will lose marks. A structured method that breaks each stage of the transaction down in time and deals with each in turn may help in this respect.

2
Consideration and promissory estoppel

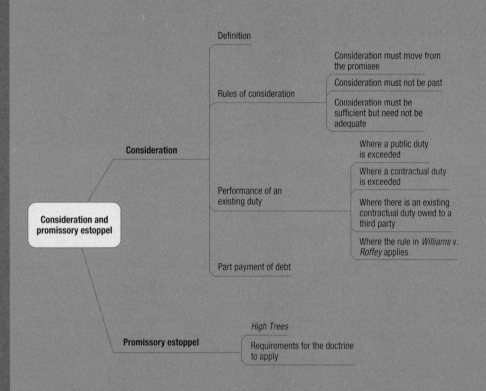

Revision Checklist

What you need to know:

- ☐ The definition of consideration
- ☐ The rules relating to 'good' consideration
- ☐ The exceptions to the general rule that performance of an existing duty is not good consideration
- ☐ The rules relating to part payment of debts
- ☐ The development and operation of promissory estoppel.

Introduction:
Consideration and promissory estoppel

Consideration is generally one of the essential elements of a binding contract.

Therefore when offer, acceptance, intention to create legal relations (Chapter 1) and consideration are present, an agreement becomes contractually binding. This chapter will review what is meant by consideration and consolidate your revision of the various rules that have developed around it. It will also look at the doctrine of promissory estoppel which is a notable exception to the general rule that promises are only binding if supported by consideration.

Essay question advice

Essay questions on consideration are relatively common. Since consideration is a topic that sets out a few basic principles, each of which has a number of exceptions, rules or modifications, then it is quite easy to set an essay which requires you to consider one or more areas within the topic and explore its rules of operation in depth. As with any essay question, it is important to have a good in-depth knowledge of the area and its supporting cases. This will enable you to demonstrate your knowledge in applying the subject matter directly to the question at hand.

Problem questions may also involve consideration. Even in a contract formation question, such as that in Chapter 1, consideration should be discussed briefly, even if it is uncontentious or unproblematic – where it is usually satisfied by the price paid in exchange for goods or services. However, you may encounter a more specific question on consideration which raises issues surrounding its timing, its adequacy or sufficiency or how it applies in cases where there is an existing contractual duty or the part payment of a debt. For these questions it is important to equip yourself with the knowledge of the rules of consideration as they apply to a particular area.

Sample question

Could you answer this question? Below is a typical essay question that could arise on this topic. Guidelines on answering the question are included at the end of the chapter, whilst a sample problem question and guidance on tackling it can be found on the Companion Website.

Essay question

To what extent does the doctrine of promissory estoppel prevent a party to a contract from enforcing their legal rights?

■ Consideration

Generally speaking, a promise is not contractually binding unless it is either made in a deed or supported by some **consideration**. English law will not enforce a gratuitous promise – therefore if I promise to clean your windows, you may only force me to do so if you have provided some consideration in return. This may be in the form of payment ('I promise to give you £10 in return for your promise to clean my windows') or some other service ('I promise to fix your washing machine in return for your promise to clean my windows'). In other words, a person to whom a promise is made (the promisee) has to give some consideration in order to render the otherwise gratuitous promise made in their favour into a legally binding contractual agreement.

Definition

The definition of consideration arises from case law.

Currie v. Misa (1875) LR 10 Ex 153

Concerning: consideration; definition

Legal principle

Lush J referred to consideration as follows:

'A valuable consideration, in the sense of the law, may consist either of some right, interest, profit or benefit accruing to the one party, or some forbearance, detriment, loss or responsibility, given, suffered or undertaken by the other.'

A more sophisticated definition was provided by Pollock in *Principles of Contract* which was approved by the House of Lords:

Dunlop v. Selfridge [1915] AC 847

Concerning: consideration; definition

Legal principle

Lord Dunedin approved Pollock's definition of consideration:

'An act of forbearance or the promise thereof is the price for which the promise of the other is bought, and the promise thus given for value is enforceable.'

Rules of consideration

There are a number of rules surrounding the operation of consideration that have built up from case law. In summary:

- consideration must move from the promisee
- consideration must not be past
- consideration must be sufficient but need not be adequate.

Consideration must move from the promisee

The rule that 'consideration must move from the promisee' means that a person to whom a promise was made can only enforce that promise if they have themselves provided the consideration for it. The promise cannot be enforced if the consideration moved from a third party.

> ### KEY CASE
>
> ### *Tweddle* v. *Atkinson* (1861) 121 ER 762
>
> **Concerning: consideration must move from the promisee**
>
> **Facts**
>
> William, the son of John Tweddle, and the daughter of William Guy intended to marry. John Tweddle agreed with William Guy in writing that both should pay money to the husband, William Tweddle. William Guy died before paying money to William Tweddle. Guy's executors refused to pay the money to Tweddle. He sued the executors to the estate.
>
> **Legal principle**
>
> William Tweddle's claim failed. Even though he was named in the agreement, he had not himself given consideration for the agreement.

This situation can be depicted in Figure 2.1.

Figure 2.1

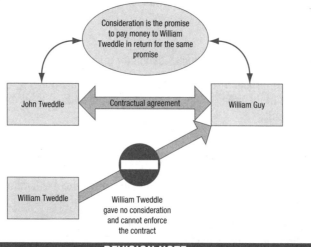

REVISION NOTE

William Tweddle was also unable to enforce the contract due to the common law rule on privity of contract. This is covered in Chapter 3. You must remember that this sort of agreement may now be subject to the Contracts (Rights of Third Parties) Act 1999, which is also considered in Chapter 3.

Consideration must not be past

To understand what this means, it is necessary to explain three different types of consideration:

■ executory consideration
■ executed consideration
■ past consideration.

Executory consideration

Executory consideration arises where promises are exchanged to perform acts in the future: for example, if I promise to deliver you an extra-large pizza and you promise to pay on delivery. This is a bilateral contract (a promise in exchange for a promise) and is enforceable: therefore if I deliver your extra-large pizza and you do not pay then I can sue you for breach of contract.

Executed consideration

Executory consideration arises where one party performs an act in order to fulfil a promise made by the other. This situation is typical of 'reward' contracts: if I offer £100 to anyone who can provide information which helps me track down my long-lost sister and you do so, then I am bound to pay you under this unilateral contract.

Past consideration

The basic principle is that the consideration for a promise must be given in return for that promise. Therefore if I clean your windows and, once I am done, you promise to pay me £10 for doing so, then I cannot enforce your promise since I did not clean your windows in return for that promise – the promise was made *after* the act was done.

KEY CASE

Re McArdle [1951] Ch 669

Concerning: past consideration

Facts

A son and his wife lived in his mother's house. On her death, the house was to pass to the son and three other children. The son's wife paid for both repairs and improvements to the property. The mother then made her four children sign an agreement to pay her daughter-in-law back from the proceeds of her estate. The mother died and the children refused to pay.

▶

Legal principle

The daughter-in-law's claim was unsuccessful. She had already performed the act before the promise to pay had been made. Therefore her consideration was past and the promise to pay was unenforceable.

It follows from this that if a guarantee is made in respect of something after it has been sold then there is no consideration for that guarantee and it is not binding (*Roscorla* v. *Thomas* (1842)).

There is an exception to the general rule that consideration must not be past:

Lampleigh v. *Braithwaite* (1615) 80 ER 255

Concerning: past consideration; exception to the general rule

Facts

Braithwaite had killed another man and asked Lampleigh to secure a pardon. Lampleigh went to considerable effort and expense to secure the pardon for Braithwaite who subsequently promised to pay Lampleigh £100. Braithwaite then failed to pay the £100. Lampleigh sued.

Legal principle

Lampleigh's claim was successful, even though, on the basis of past consideration, his efforts were in the past in relation to the promise to pay. The court, however, considered that the original request by Braithwaite in fact contained an implied promise that he would reward and reimburse Lampleigh for his efforts: therefore the previous request and the subsequent promise were part of the same transaction and were enforceable.

Therefore if services are rendered on request and where both parties understand that payment will be made, the promise may be enforceable even though the consideration is past. The principle was affirmed in *Re Casey's Patents* (1892) with the criteria being restated by Lord Scarman in *Pao On* v. *Lau Yiu Long* (1980) as follows:

- The act must have been done at the promisor's request.
- The parties must have understood that the act was to be remunerated further by a payment or the conferment of some other benefit and payment (in other words, an implied promise to pay to be quantified at a later date).
- The payment, or the conferment of a benefit, must have been legally enforceable had it been promised in advance.

Consideration must be sufficient but need not be adequate

As long as the consideration has some value (sufficient to render the promise enforceable) the courts will not concern themselves with its adequacy (whether it represents a good bargain). For instance, if I freely decide to offer to sell you my brand new camera for 20p and you accept then this is sufficient to render the contract binding even though it is seemingly not a fair exchange.

KEY CASE

***Thomas* v. *Thomas* (1842) 2 QB 851**

Concerning: sufficiency and adequacy of consideration

Facts
A husband expressed a wish that his wife should be allowed to remain in their house after his death. This was not written in his will. After his death, his executors allowed his wife to stay at a rent of £1 per year. They later tried to dispossess her.

Legal principle
The payment of the 'peppercorn' rent was sufficient consideration for the contract to be enforceable. The husband's wish alone, however, would not have been sufficient consideration for the contract to be enforceable.

In order to be sufficient in law, consideration must be:

▌ real
▌ tangible
▌ valuable (that is, it must have some actual value).

FURTHER THINKING

Consideration is straightforward when the value is pecuniary, i.e. can be expressed in terms of a sum of money, but this is not the only way in which something can be viewed as valuable. For example, in *White* v. *Bluett* (1853) a son attempted to claim that he did not owe his late father's estate repayment of a sum of money due on a promissory note since he had agreed with his father that the debt would be written off in return for his promise not to complain about his father's will. This promise not to complain was held to be insufficiently tangible to amount to good consideration. However, in *Ward* v. *Byham* (1956) a mother's promise to keep her illegitimate child 'well looked after and happy' in return for money towards the child's upkeep from its father was held to be sufficient consideration (since there is no legal duty to keep a child happy). In some instances, apparently worthless items have been held to be good consideration.

KEY CASE

Chappell & Co. Ltd v. *Nestlé Co. Ltd* [1960] AC 87

Concerning: sufficiency and adequacy of consideration

Facts

Nestlé were offering a record (the copyright of which was owned by Chappell) for sale at 1s. 6d **plus** three wrappers from their chocolate bars. The record normally sold at 6s. 8d. Permission to use the copyright was not obtained. Chappell sued to prevent the promotion since they would receive a much lower royalty from it.

Legal principle

The wrappers were held to be part of the consideration, even though they were thrown away when received. As Lord Somervell commented:

> 'It is said that, when received, the wrappers are of no value to Nestlé. This is irrelevant. A contracting party can stipulate for what consideration he chooses. A peppercorn does not cease to be good consideration if it is established that the promisee does not like pepper and will throw away the corn.'

Performance of an existing duty

In general, if a party is performing a duty which he is already bound to do then this is not sufficient to amount to consideration for a new agreement. In essence, since consideration is defined in terms of a detriment or forbearance, then it seems logical that you cannot suffer any detriment in relation to a new promise if that detriment is something that you were going to have to do anyway.

This applies to public as well as contractual duties:

KEY CASE

Collins v. *Godefroy* (1831) 109 ER 1040

Concerning: consideration; performance of an existing public duty

Facts

A police officer was promised a sum of money by the defendant in a trial in return for the officer giving evidence, since it was important to the defendant that the officer did so. The officer had already been subpoenaed to do so.

KEY CASE

Legal principle

The promise to pay was unenforceable since there was no consideration given by the police officer for it. He was already under a legal duty to attend court.

KEY CASE

***Stilk* v. *Myrick* (1809) 170 ER 1168**

Concerning: consideration; performance of an existing contractual duty

Facts

A team of eleven sailors agreed to crew a ship from London to the Baltic and back. Two sailors deserted in the Baltic. The remaining nine refused to work, and pressed the captain for higher wages. He agreed at the time but ultimately refused to pay. The sailors sued the captain.

Legal principle

The promise to pay was unenforceable since the sailors were already contractually bound to return the ship to London. Therefore there was no consideration given by the sailors in return for the captain's promise to pay additional wages.

Therefore, the basic rule in relation to performance of an existing duty is that it is not good consideration for a new promise.

However, there are exceptions to this basic rule:

- where a public duty is exceeded
- where a contractual duty is exceeded
- where there is an existing contractual duty owed to a third party
- where the rule in *Williams* v. *Roffey* (see page 42) applies.

Where a public duty is exceeded

KEY CASE

***Glassbrook Bros* v. *Glamorgan County Council* [1925] AC 270**

Concerning: consideration; exceeding an existing public duty

Facts

During a miners' strike, the owner of a pit asked the police for extra protection and promised to pay for it. After the strike, the pit owner refused to pay, claiming that the police were already bound by a public duty to protect the pit.

> **KEY CASE**
>
> **Legal principle**
>
> The promise to pay was enforceable: since the police had done more than they would ordinarily have done (in sending additional officers), this was good consideration for the pit owner's promise to pay.

Therefore, if one party ends up giving more than they would otherwise have done, then this *additional* detriment represents sufficient consideration to render a promise given in return for it enforceable. The same principle also applies to contractual duties.

Where a contractual duty is exceeded

> **KEY CASE**
>
> *Hartley* v. *Ponsonby* (1857) 7 E & B 872
>
> **Concerning: consideration; exceeding an existing contractual duty**
>
> **Facts**
>
> The facts of this case are very similar to *Stilk* v. *Myrick* and involved a number of sailors deserting a ship. The captain had promised to pay the remaining sailors additional wages for crewing his ship back home. However, in *Stilk* v. *Myrick* 9 crew out of 11 remained; in this case 19 out of 36 remained.
>
> **Legal principle**
>
> The promise to pay was enforceable: the court considered that the greater proportional reduction in crew numbers (in this case almost half the crew deserted, rather than 2 from 11) made the return voyage much more dangerous since the ship was short-handed. The sailors' promise to return under more dangerous conditions had exceeded their existing contractual obligations and therefore this represented good consideration for the promise of extra pay.

Again, the principle appears to be that where a party does more than that for which they originally bargained, then this is good consideration to support a fresh bargain. This has also been applied in circumstances involving third parties.

Where there is an existing contractual duty owed to a third party

The performance (or promise to perform) an existing contractual duty owed by the promisee to a third party is also good consideration.

KEY CASE

Scotson v. *Pegg* (1861) 6 H & N 295

Concerning: consideration; performance of an existing contractual duty owed to a third party

Facts

Scotson contracted to deliver coal to X, or to X's order. X sold the coal to Pegg and ordered Scotson to deliver the coal to Pegg. Pegg promised Scotson that he would unload it at a fixed daily rate. Pegg did not fulfil this promise. Scotson attempted to enforce Pegg's promise. Pegg argued that the promise was not binding because Scotson had not provided consideration as Scotson was bound by his contract with X (a third party) to deliver the coal.

Legal principle

It was held that delivery of the coal to Pegg (in other words, the performance of the existing contractual duty owed to X by Scotson) was good consideration to enforce Pegg's promise to pay.

The facts of *Scotson* v. *Pegg* are best illustrated by a diagram (Figure 2.2).

Figure 2.2

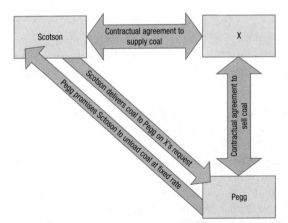

The decision in *Scotson* v. *Pegg* has been approved by the Privy Council in *Pao On* v. *Lau Yiu Long* (1980) and *New Zealand Shipping Co. Ltd* v. *A. M. Satterthwaite & Co. Ltd (The Eurymedon)* (1975).

Where the rule in *Williams* v. *Roffey* applies

The most recent 'refinement and limitation' to the rule in *Stilk* v. *Myrick* was made in *Williams* v. *Roffey Bros & Nicholls (Contractors) Ltd* (1991):

Williams v. *Roffey Bros & Nicholls (Contractors) Ltd* [1991] 1 QB 1

Concerning: consideration; extra benefit

Facts

Roffey Bros was a firm of builders contracted to renovate a block of flats. Their own contract contained a penalty clause for late completion, so it was in their interests to finish the work on time. They sub-contracted the carpentry work to Williams for £20,000. Williams fell behind schedule because, they claimed, they had not quoted a high enough price for the work. Roffey promised to pay Williams an additional sum of £10,300 to complete the carpentry on time. When the work was complete, Roffey refused to pay, claiming that the new agreement with Williams was void for lack of consideration (since Williams were already fulfilling a contractual obligation).

Legal principle

The Court of Appeal held that Williams had provided consideration by completing the work on time and therefore Roffey's promise to pay the additional £10,300 was binding, even though, at first glance, this proposition seemed incompatible with the rule from *Stilk* v. *Myrick.*

Glidewell LJ explained that this case refined and limited the application of the principle from *Stilk* v. *Myrick* but left the basic principle intact. Following *Ward* v. *Byham* and *Pao On*, he stated that the present state of the law on this subject can be expressed in the following proposition:

(i)   if A has entered into a contract with B to do work for, or to supply goods or services to, B in return for payment by B; and

(ii) at some stage before A has completely performed his obligations under the contract B has reason to doubt whether A will, or will be able to, complete his side of the bargain; and

(iii) B thereupon promises A an additional payment in return for A's promise to perform his contractual obligations on time; and

(iv) as a result of giving his promise, B obtains in practice a benefit, or obviates a disbenefit; and

(v)   B's promise is not given as a result of economic duress or fraud on the part of A; then

(vi) the benefit to B is capable of being consideration for B's promise, so that the promise will be legally binding.

Following this proposition, the court considered that the practical benefit to Roffey was the avoidance of the penalty clause and, moreover, that the arrangement with

Williams meant that they did not have to find another carpenter. This practical benefit was sufficient consideration for the promise to pay extra to Williams to complete what he was already bound to do under the existing contract.

EXAM TIP

If a problem question involves a situation where one party to a contractual agreement is desperate (for whatever reason) for the other party to complete their promise on time then this is a good clue that a discussion of *Williams* v. *Roffey* will be required.

Part payment of debt

The basic common law rule relating to part payment of a debt was stated in *Pinnel's Case* (1602)

KEY CASE

Pinnel's Case (1602) 5 Co Rep 117a

Concerning: consideration; part payment of a debt

Facts

Cole owed Pinnel £8 10s. At Pinnel's request, Cole paid £5 2s. 6d. one month before the full sum was due. Cole claimed that there was an agreement that the part payment would discharge the full debt.

Legal principle

Pinnel was unsuccessful in claiming the balance of the unpaid debt. The court held that in general part payment of an original debt did not provide good consideration for the promise to waive the balance. However, since Pinnel gained some benefit by part payment having been made early, this was sufficient consideration to enforce his promise to forego the balance of the debt. The court stated that:

'Payment of a lesser sum on the day in satisfaction of a greater sum cannot be any satisfaction for the whole, because it appears to the Judges that by no possibility, a lesser sum can be a satisfaction to the [claimant] for a greater sum: but the gift of a horse, hawk, or robe, etc. in satisfaction is good ... [as] more beneficial to the [claimant] than the money.'

Therefore, payment of a lesser sum may discharge the full debt if some additional consideration is provided. This may be so if the part payment is made:

- before it is due (as in *Pinnel's Case*);
- by different means (for instance, if the creditor agrees to accept some property in lieu of money – even if this is worth less than the value of the debt: remember that consideration does not need to be adequate);
- in a different place to that originally specified.

These situations provide sufficient consideration in terms of a benefit to the creditor and a detriment to the debtor.

However, the rule from *Pinnel's Case* can operate harshly:

KEY CASE

***Foakes* v. *Beer* (1884) 9 App Cas 605**

Concerning: consideration; part payment of a debt

Facts

Foakes owed Beer £2,090. They agreed that Foakes could pay in instalments. Beer agreed that no further action would be taken if the debt was paid by the agreed date. Later, Beer demanded an additional interest payment. Foakes refused to pay.

Legal principle

Beer succeeded in the claim for the interest payment. The same reasoning was applied as in *Pinnel's Case*.

The decision in *Foakes* v. *Beer* appears unfair to Foakes since he had relied on Beer's promise not to take further action if the debt was repaid. It is the potential harshness of the common law rule (which remains good law) which led to the development of the equitable doctrine of promissory estoppel.

Promissory estoppel

The equitable doctrine of promissory estoppel can provide a means of making a promise binding, even without consideration. It was developed from Lord Denning's *obiter* statement:

KEY CASE

***Central London Property Trust* v. *High Trees House Ltd* [1947] KB 130**

Concerning: promissory estoppel

Facts

In 1937 High Trees House Ltd leased a block of flats at the rate £2,500 per year from Central London Property Trust Ltd. Due to the war, occupancy rates

---

were drastically lower than normal. In January 1940, the parties agreed in writing to reduce the rent by half. Neither party stipulated the period for which this reduced rent was to apply. High Trees paid the reduced rate for five years as the flats began to fill and by 1945 the flats were full. Central London Property Trust sued for payment of the full rental costs from July 1945 onwards.

Legal principle

The court considered *Hughes* v. *Metropolitan Railway Co.* (1877) which concerned the doctrine of waiver – that is, that parties should be prevented from going back on a promise to waive certain rights. In this case, Lord Denning held that the full rent was payable from the time that the flats became fully occupied in mid-1945. He also stated *obiter* that if Central London had tried to claim for the full rent from 1940 onwards, they would not have been able to. They would be estopped (i.e. prevented) from reneging on the promise upon which the defendants had relied upon as long as the circumstances which led to that promise continued.

The doctrine of promissory estoppel applies subject to certain requirements:

- there must be a clear or unequivocal promise or representation (*Collin* v. *Duke of Westminster* (1985));
- which is intended to affect the legal relationship between the parties (*Spence* v. *Shell* (1980)); and
- which indicates that the promisor will not insist upon his strict legal rights against the promisee in relation to the promise;
- the promise or representation must have influenced the conduct of the promisee in some way (it is often said that the promisee must have acted in reliance upon that promise) (*W J Alan Co. Ltd* v. *El Nasr Export and Import Co.* (1972));
- it must be inequitable for the promisor to go back on the promise (*D & C Builders* v. *Rees* (1965));
- the doctrine can only be used as a defence. Since it is an equitable doctrine, the general equitable maxim that 'equity is a shield, not a sword' applies. It does not create new rights (*Combe* v. *Combe* (1951));
- the doctrine temporarily suspends rights; it does not extinguish them (*Tool Metal Manufacturing Co.* v. *Tungsten Electric Co. Ltd* (1955));
- since it is an equitable doctrine, it is available only at the discretion of the court.

FURTHER THINKING

It appears unlikely that the doctrine will be developed further. In *Brikom Investments* v. *Carr* (1979) Roskill LJ stated that 'it would be wrong to extend the doctrine of promissory estoppel ... to the extent of abolishing in this back-handed way the doctrine of consideration': in particular, an attempt to rely on *Williams* v. *Roffey* in situations involving part payment of debt failed (*Re Selectmove* (1995)). You might find it helpful to read around this topic to develop your understanding. Halliwell, M., 'Estoppel: Unconscionability as a Cause of Action' (1994) 14 *Legal Studies* 15 provides a detailed analysis of the role of estoppel that would help you to prepare for an essay on this topic.

Chapter Summary:
Putting it all together

TEST YOURSELF

- [ ] Can you tick all the points from the revision checklist at the beginning of this chapter?
- [ ] Take the **end-of-chapter quiz** on the Companion Website.
- [ ] Test your knowledge of the cases below with the **revision flashcards** on the website.
- [ ] Attempt the essay question from the beginning of the chapter using the guidelines below.
- [ ] Go to the Companion Website to try out other questions.

Answer guidelines

See the essay question at the start of the chapter.

Points to remember when answering this question:
- This question requires a discussion of the relationship between the doctrine of promissory estoppel and the role of consideration in the part payment of a debt.
- You could start by explaining the common law rule from *Pinnel's Case* – that part payment of a debt on the due date can never satisfy the full debt owed, but if some additional consideration is given then this may render a promise to forego the balance binding. You could mention *Foakes* v. *Beer* and *Re Selectmove* in support of this.
- You should explain that the common law rule can lead to harsh outcomes and the doctrine of promissory estoppel was developed in order to mitigate some of the harshness of the common law.
- You should discuss the origins of the doctrine from *Hughes* v. *Metropolitan Railway* and its development by Lord Denning in *High Trees*.
- You should also discuss, with supporting case authority, the conditions which must be satisfied for the doctrine to operate.

■ Finally, you should draw together the various strands of your argument to reach a conclusion. In summary, the doctrine of promissory estoppel will prevent the enforcement of strict legal rights in certain circumstances, provided that the criteria required for its operation are met.

Make your answer really stand out:

■ As with many areas of contract law, this particular topic is heavily based on case law. You should therefore endeavour to support as many statements of law with case authority as you can.

■ You must take care to answer the question asked, rather than writing all you know about promissory estoppel. Take time and care to relate the points that you make back to the question that is asked. This will maintain focus.

■ In a question of this nature, many students forget to discuss that promissory estoppel is an *equitable* doctrine: therefore it is available only at the discretion of the court and may be used only as a 'shield not a sword'. A discussion of the doctrine's equitable nature will demonstrate good understanding.

3
Contracts and third parties

Privity of contract

- The general rule
- Exceptions provided by statute
- Collateral contracts
- Agency
- Covenants in land law
  - Restrictive covenants
  - Covenants in leases
- Trusts
- The right to claim damages

Contracts and third parties

Contracts (Rights of Third Parties) Act 1999

- Statutory third party rights
- Exceptions
- Variation of the contract
- Remedies for third parties

A printable version of this topic map is available from www.pearsoned.co.uk/lawexpress

Revision Checklist

What you need to know:

☐ The operation of the general doctrine of privity of contract

☐ The various exceptions to the general doctrine of privity

☐ The circumstances in which a third party to a contract may recover damages

☐ The main provisions of the Contracts (Rights of Third Parties) Act 1999 and their effects

☐ The remedies that are available to a third party under the Contracts (Rights of Third Parties) Act 1999.

Introduction:
Contracts and third parties

In some situations, third parties to contracts may still acquire rights and liabilities under them, even if they are not party to the agreement themselves.

This chapter will start with the basic principle: that third parties may not enforce the terms of a contract to which they are not a party. However, there are many exceptions to the basic doctrine of privity of contract which have attempted to mitigate some of the potentially harsh outcomes that might result from its strict application. Once the position at common law has been investigated, the chapter will finally turn to consider the statutory reform of the area introduced by the Contracts (Rights of Third Parties) Act 1999 and will describe the effect of its most significant provisions.

Essay question advice

Since this topic has a relatively unsatisfactory common law position which has resulted in both the development of a large number of common law exceptions and statutory reform it is the sort of topic that lends itself to essay questions. Such questions will require a comprehensive knowledge and understanding of the various exceptions, the cases in which they arose and some of the underlying reasons as to why the courts decided to deviate from the general position in each case. You should also ensure that you are familiar with the key provisions of the Contracts (Rights of Third Parties) Act 1999 both in terms of their operation and the effect that they might have had on earlier cases if the Act had been in force at the time.

It is probably unlikely that an entire problem question would be set on privity of contract. However, it is the sort of topic that could be mixed in with other areas of contract law and therefore a good working knowledge of the operation of this area is important. Even though the Contracts (Rights of Third Parties) Act 1999 is now in force, do not be tempted to discount the value of the common law position. You may be asked to advise one of the parties as to their position at common law as well as under statute, or be given a set of facts to discuss with a part question asking you if your answer would be any different if the events in the problem scenario took place before the Act was in force.

Sample question

Could you answer this question? Below is a typical essay question that could arise on this topic. Guidelines on answering the question are included at the end of the chapter, whilst a sample problem question and guidance on tackling it can be found on the Companion Website.

Essay question

Where a contract confers a benefit on a third party, it is enforceable by the third party in their own right.

Discuss.

■ Privity of contract

The general rule

The general rule of privity of contract is that only parties to a contract can acquire rights and liabilities under that contract. It follows that if you are not a party to a contract then you cannot sue upon it, or be sued under it.

KEY CASE

***Dunlop* v. *Selfridge* [1915] AC 847**

Concerning: privity of contract

Facts

Dunlop sold tyres to Dew & Co. who were wholesalers. Dew & Co. undertook (expressly in the contract) that the manufacturers could fix the lowest price at

---

▶

which they could sell the tyre and promised not to sell the tyres below that price. Dew & Co. also agreed to obtain the same pricing terms from customers to whom they resold the tyres. They sold tyres to Selfridge on these terms. Selfridge broke the pricing agreement and sold the tyres at discount prices. Dunlop sued Selfridge and sought an injunction to prevent them from selling their tyres at a discount.

Legal principle

Dunlop failed. Although there was a contract between them and Dew & Co., Selfridge were not a party to that contract and Dunlop could not therefore impose their terms upon them.

REVISION NOTE

Dunlop v. *Selfridge* also contained Lord Dunedin's approval of Pollock's definition of consideration. See Chapter 2.

In questions involving privity, it is often useful to sketch out a diagram showing where the various contractual relationships lie. For example *Dunlop* v. *Selfridge* could be depicted as shown in Figure 3.1 overleaf.

REVISION NOTE

Tweddle v. *Atkinson* which was covered in Chapter 2 also involved privity of contract. Here the attempt by the third party to enforce the contract which conferred a benefit upon him failed on the rule of privity as well as failing for lack of consideration.

The common law rule of privity has been criticised for leading to harsh and unfair outcomes, particularly in cases where the contract purports to confer a benefit on a third party who remains unable to sue if that benefit is not forthcoming due to a breach by one of the parties to the contract (this was the situation in *Tweddle* v. *Atkinson*). Therefore a number of exceptions to the basic rule have been developed:

- exceptions provided by statute
- collateral contracts
- agency
- covenants in land law
- trusts.

Figure 3.1

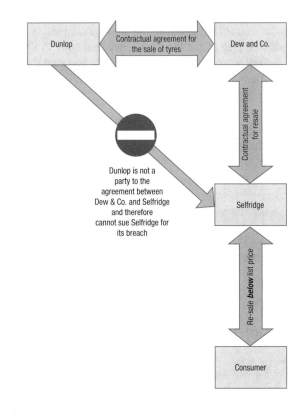

FURTHER THINKING

The basic doctrine of privity has been criticised in a number of cases. Look at the judgments in *Beswick* v. *Beswick* (1968), *Jackson* v. *Horizon Holidays Ltd* (1975); *Woodar Investment Development Ltd* v. *Wimpey Construction (UK) Ltd* (1980) and *Darlington Borough Council* v. *Wiltshier Northern Ltd* (1995) and summarise the judicial criticisms put forward. This depth of knowledge would come in useful for an essay question on privity.

Exceptions provided by statute

Statutory exceptions to the rule include the following:

Statutory provision	Effect
Section 148(7) Road Traffic Act 1988	Requires drivers to have third party insurance which can be relied upon by third parties who suffer loss or damage even though they are not a party to that contract
Section 11 Married Women's Property Act 1882	Allows a wife to claim on her husband's life assurance policy
Section 29 Bills of Exchange Act 1882	A third party may sue on a cheque or bill of exchange
Section 136 Law of Property Act 1925	Allows rights arising under a contract to be assigned to a third party
Section 56(1) Law of Property Act 1925	Allows a person to acquire an interest in land or other property or the benefit of a covenant relating to land or other property even if that person is not expressly named in the conveyance (or other document)
Competition Act 1998	Prohibits price-fixing arrangements (such as those in *Dunlop* v. *Selfridge*)

However, attempts to use statute as a creative 'loophole' to avoid the basic doctrine of privity have failed (see, for example, *Beswick* v. *Beswick* (1968) which concerned the use of section 56(1) of the Law of Property Act 1925 in relation to personal property rather than to land or an interest in land).

Collateral contracts

A collateral contract may be used to avoid the rule relating to privity. In essence a contract between two parties may be accompanied by a collateral contact between one of those parties and a third party *relating to the same subject matter.*

Shanklin Pier v. *Detel Products Ltd* [1951] AC 847

Concerning: privity of contract

Facts

The claimants entered into a contract with painting contractors to paint their pier, having been assured by the defendants (paint manufacturers) that their paint would last for at least seven years without deterioration. The defendants then sold the paint to the contractors. However, the paint peeled within three months. The pier owners could not sue the painters since they had carried out the work professionally and thus had completed their side of the contract. The pier owners sued the paint manufacturers.

Legal principle

The pier owners were successful. Although they were not a party to the contract between the paint manufacturers and the painting contractors (and therefore there was no privity of contract) it was held that a collateral contract had arisen from their promise as to the suitability of the paint.

The collateral contract device can be seen as a way to identify a contract between the party making a promise (Detel) and the other party (Shanklin Pier) since this promise has induced the other party (Shanklin Pier) to enter into a separate contract with a different party (the painting contractors). Therefore, the party making the promise (Detel) gains some benefit in being able to sell their goods (paint) on the strength of the 'main' contract (between Shanklin Pier and the painting contractors) and are held to be bound by their promise (see Figure 3.2).

Figure 3.2

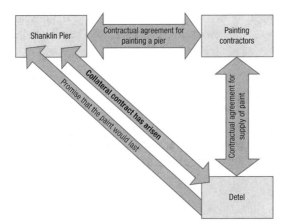

Strictly speaking the use of a collateral contract is not an exception to the doctrine of privity, since a new contract arises. However, it is an effective means of evading the doctrine of privity.

Agency

The contract of agency is a common law exception to the doctrine of privity. The parties in an agency arrangement are as follows:

Party	Description
Principal	The party on whose behalf the contract is made and who receives the benefit arising under the contract.
Agent	The agent is a party to the contract with the third party. The agent has a direct contractual relationship with the third party, but is making the contract on behalf of the principal and not on his own behalf.
Third party	The third party enters into the contract with the agent. However, the rules of agency provide that there is no contractual relationship with the agent. Instead the principal is bound by the contractual relationship with the third party which has been entered into by the agent on his behalf.

The relationship between these three parties can be depicted as shown in Figure 3.3.

Figure 3.3

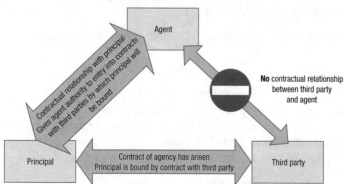

Covenants in land law

A covenant is an agreement between two or more parties made in the form of a deed. It is therefore similar to a contract, with the exception that contracts made by deed do not have to be supported by consideration.

REVISION NOTE

This section covers only the very basic details of land law sufficient to illustrate the points relating to privity of contract. If you have already studied land law, it might be useful to look back at your materials on restrictive covenants and leases to refresh your memory on the principles before proceeding to cover the rest of this section.

Restrictive covenants

In land law, in certain circumstances, covenants can 'run with the land'. If, for example, Tom, a builder, builds a row of houses, and sells them to Chris, Becky and Tricia, he can enter into a covenant with each of them in which they promise not to block the shared drains. However, if Becky sells her house to Sanjay, then Sanjay and Tom are not parties to any contract. Therefore if Sanjay blocks the shared drain, under the doctrine of privity, Tom could not sue Sanjay because they are not parties to the covenant (contract). Chris and Tricia also have no contractual relationship with Sanjay, even though they are suffering from blocked drains as a result of his actions.

In order to address this situation, an equitable device has developed which means that *restrictive covenants* (promises to refrain from doing something) will, if properly created, bind successive purchasers of the land even though there is no privity between them and the original seller.

KEY CASE

Tulk v. *Moxhay* (1848) 41 ER 1143

Concerning: privity of contract; restrictive covenants over land

Facts

Tulk owned land which he sold subject to an express promise that it would not be used for property development. The land was re-sold several times, subject to the same undertaking. Moxhay eventually bought the land and, despite knowing of the restriction, intended to build upon it. Tulk sought an injunction to prevent Moxhay from building on the land.

▶

> **KEY CASE**
>
> **Legal principle**
>
> Tulk's claim was successful. The court considered that it would be unconscionable for Moxhay to buy with knowledge of the restriction and yet to build on the land. An injunction was therefore granted to enforce the original agreement between Tulk and the first purchaser of the land, even though Moxhay had not been a party to that agreement.

This principle applies subject to two conditions:

▌ the third party must have had notice of the restrictive covenant at the time of purchase; and

▌ the original seller must have retained land which was capable of benefiting from the restriction.

However, the principle from *Tulk* v. *Moxhay* generally only applies to land. It certainly failed in relation to a price-fixing arrangement (similar to that in *Dunlop* v. *Selfridge*) in *Taddy* v. *Sterious* (1904). However, in *Lord Strathcona Steamship Co.* v. *Dominion Coal Co.* (1926), the Privy Council applied the principle in relation to the use of a ship that had been sold with notice of a charter. This decision was criticised on the basis that the third party did not have any proprietary interest as required by *Tulk* v. *Moxhay* and its use has been restricted since. In *Clore* v. *Theatrical Properties Ltd* (1936) it was held that the decision in *Strathcona* should be used only in the particular circumstances relating to ship's charters. *Port Line Ltd* v. *Ben Line Steamers Ltd* (1958) went further in stating that *Strathcona* was wrongly decided.

Covenants in leases

Where a landlord grants a lease to another person, there are typically various covenants contained within the lease. There is privity of contract between the landlord and tenant and the terms of the lease are enforceable by both. The landlord may also enforce those covenants against anyone to whom the lease is assigned (sold). Sections 141 and 142 of the Law of Property Act 1925 also provide that a tenant may be able to enforce covenants against a new landlord (if the freehold is sold) and vice versa that the new landlord may enforce those covenants against the tenant. However, if the lessee sub-lets the property, then the landlord will have no privity with the sub-tenant (see Figure 3.4 overleaf).

Figure 3.4

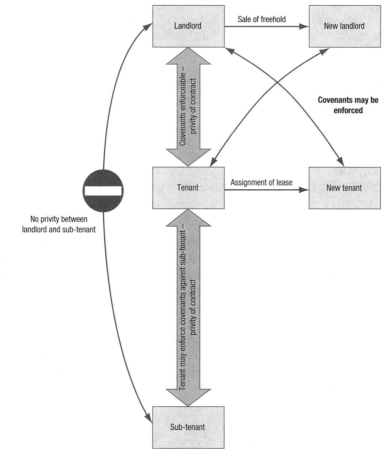

Trusts

As with the previous section on land law, this section carries limited discussion of the fundamentals of trusts. If you have already studied equity and trusts you should take some time to re-equip yourself with the basics before looking at the specific application of trusts to privity in the rest of this section.

The doctrine of privity may also be avoided in the situation where one of the parties to a contract which confers a benefit on a third party holds their contractual rights in trust for that third party. This can be depicted as shown in Figure 3.5.

Figure 3.5

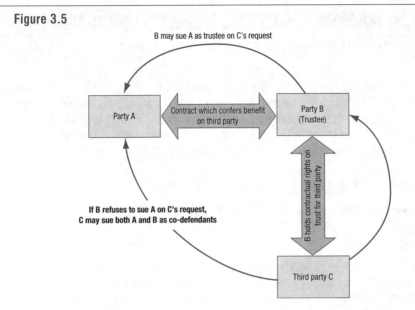

This principle was established in *Gregory & Parker* v. *Williams* (1817) and affirmed in *Les Affréteurs Réunis SA* v. *Walford* (1919). In order for the principle to apply there must be an express intention in the contract between A and B that C should receive a benefit and a trust will be found only if the court considers that the interest is compatible with the general principles of trust law (*Green* v. *Russell* (1959)).

REVISION NOTE

Remember that the use of trusts in an attempt to circumvent the doctrine of privity is a creation of the law of trusts rather than the law of contract. It is included here to demonstrate how creative parties have had to become in order to find ways around seemingly harsh and rigid applications of the basic doctrine.

The right to claim damages

Unless one of the exceptions to the doctrine of privity arises, then the third party has no means of enforcing the contract at common law unless one of the parties to the contract sues in their own right. However, if the contract confers a benefit on the third party, it is unlikely that the party who brings the claim will have suffered loss themselves. Therefore, if an award of damages is made, strictly speaking, this will be to compensate the party who brings the claim, who – having suffered no loss – would be entitled to only nominal damages.

REVISION NOTE

The remedy of nominal damages is discussed further in Chapter 9.

However, there is a common law rule originating from the shipping case of *Dunlop* v. *Lambert* (1839) which allows a remedy to be awarded to a party even without privity of contract 'where no other would be available to a person sustaining loss which under a rational legal system ought to be compensated by the person who caused it'.

This rule was applied broadly in relation to a family holiday:

KEY CASE

Jackson v. *Horizon Holidays Ltd* [1975] 1 WLR 1468

Concerning: privity of contract: recovery by third parties

Facts

Jackson had booked a family holiday in his sole name. For a variety of reasons, the holiday was a complete travesty: the accommodation, food, services, facilities and general standard of the hotel to which they were transported proved so unsatisfactory that the whole family suffered discomfort, vexation, inconvenience and distress and went home disappointed. Jackson sued the holiday company on his own behalf and that of his family. The company disputed that they should pay damages in respect of the family since they were not parties to the contract.

Legal principle

The Court of Appeal held that the disappointment suffered by the family was a loss to Jackson himself and awarded damages in respect of the whole family on that basis.

This decision was criticised as being of too wide an application and was narrowed by the House of Lords.

KEY CASE

Woodar Investment Development Ltd v. *Wimpey Construction (UK) Ltd* [1980] 1 WLR 277

Concerning: privity of contract: recovery by third parties

Facts

The purchasers, Wimpey Construction, had entered into a contract to buy certain land from the vendors, Woodar. The purchase price was £850,000 of which £150,000 was to be paid on completion to Transworld Trade, a third

---

KEY CASE

party. The sale was to complete within two months of planning permission for the site being granted or a fixed date (whichever was the earlier). Wimpey unlawfully repudiated the contract after the market fell.

Legal principle

The issue here concerned whether damages should include the £150,000 payable to the third party. Although the House of Lords did not overrule *Jackson*, it was held that there was no general principle allowing a party to a contract to sue on behalf of a third party who had suffered loss as a result of breach of that contract.

It appeared, then, that the relaxation of the doctrine was not of general utility and that its use had been specifically restricted by the House to Lords to holiday contracts. However, the principle from *Dunlop* v. *Lambert* was extended to property as well as carriage of goods in *Linden Gardens Trust Ltd* v. *Lanesta Sludge Disposals Ltd* (1994) and most recently considered (although not clarified) by the House of Lords in *Alfred McAlpine Construction Ltd* v. *Panatown Ltd* (2001):

KEY CASE

Alfred McAlpine Construction Ltd v. *Panatown Ltd* [2001] 1 AC 518

Concerning: privity of contract: recovery by third parties

Facts

There was a contract between McAlpine and Panatown for the design and build of a multi-storey car park. McAlpine had also entered into a 'duty of care' deed with Unex Investment Properties Ltd (UIPL) who were the owners of the site. By that deed UIPL acquired a direct remedy against McAlpine in respect of any failure by the contractor to exercise reasonable skill, care and attention to any matter within the scope of the contractor's responsibilities under the contract. The deed was expressly assignable by the owner to its successors in title. Serious defects were found in the building and Panatown sued.

Legal principle

The House of Lords held that the duty of care deed with the third party (UIPL) prevented Panatown from suing since this deed gave the third party a specific remedy. However, the Lords were split 3 – 2 on the issue which suggests that the law is still somewhat unclear in this area.

The common law position was amended by statute in the form of the Contracts (Rights of Third Parties) Act 1999.

■ Contracts (Rights of Third Parties) Act 1999

As you have seen, there are a number of exceptions to the general doctrine of privity of contract. This suggests that the courts have been far from content with the strict operation of the doctrine. The increasing number of exceptions led to this area of law becoming more complicated, and it is not surprising that there have been several calls for legislative reform. Following a Law Commission consultation, a draft Bill was presented to Parliament which ultimately became the Contracts (Rights of Third Parties) Act 1999.

Statutory third party rights

The main changes to the common law position are found in section 1 of the Act.

KEY STATUTE

Contracts (Rights of Third Parties) Act 1999, section 1(1) – (3)

'1. – (1) Subject to the provisions of this Act, a person who is not a party to a contract (a "third party") may in his own right enforce a term of the contract if –
  (a) the contract expressly provides that he may, or
  (b) subject to subsection (2), the term purports to confer a benefit on him.

(2) Subsection (1)(b) does not apply if on a proper construction of the contract it appears that the parties did not intend the term to be enforceable by the third party.

(3) The third party must be expressly identified in the contract by name, as a member of a class or as answering a particular description but need not be in existence when the contract is entered into.'

Therefore the Act allows contractual provisions to be enforced by a non-contracting party in two circumstances:

- where the contract *expressly* provides that he may (section 1(1)(a)),
- where the contract term purports to confer a benefit upon him (section 1(1)(b)),
- *provided that* it appears that the parties did not intend the term to be enforceable by the third party (section 1(2)).

In *Nisshin Shipping Co. Ltd* v. *Cleaves & Co. Ltd* (2003) the interpretation of the Act was tested in court for the first time. It was held that if the contract is neutral on the question of whether the term was intended to be enforceable by the third party then section 1(2) does not disapply section 1(1)(b).

Section 1(3) provides that the party must be identified by name, as a member of a class or answering a particular description but need not exist when the contract is entered into. This could extend rights to unborn children, a future spouse or a company which was not incorporated at the time of formation of the contract.

Exceptions

The Act will not apply to:

∎ bills of exchange, promissory notes and negotiable instruments (section 6(1))
∎ statutory contracts that were made under section 14 of the Companies Act 1985 (now repealed by the Companies Act 2006) (section 6(2))
∎ any incorportion document of a limited liability partnership or any limited liability partnership agreement (section 6(2A))
∎ contracts of employment (section 6(3))
∎ contracts for the carriage of goods by sea (other than clauses of exclusion or limitation) (section 6(4)).

Variation of the contract

The promised benefit to the third party may not be removed by a variation of the contract if:

∎ the third party has communicated his assent to the term to the promisor (section 2(1)(a)),
∎ the promisor is aware that the third party has relied on the term (section 2(1)(b)), or
∎ the promisor can reasonably be expected to have foreseen that the third party would rely on the term and the third party has in fact relied on it (section 2(1)(c)).

Remedies for third parties

Section 1(5) of the Act provides that the third party has available to him any remedy that would have been available to him in an action for breach of contract if he had been a party to the contract. The rules relating to damages, injunctions, specific performance and other relief apply in the same way as if he had been a party to the contract. However, if the promisee has already recovered damages from the promisor in respect of losses suffered by the third party, then section 5 will operate to reduce any award to the third party to take account of damages already recovered from the promisor. This provision operates to prevent the promisor from double liability to both the promisee and the third party.

The impact of the Contracts (Rights of Third Parties) Act 1999 on the traditional doctrine of privity is an important issue in contract law and, as such, has the potential to form the basis of an essay question. Andrews, N., 'Strangers to Justice No Longer: the Reversal of the Privity Rule Under the Contracts (Rights of Third Parties) Act 1999' (2001) 60 *Cambridge Law Journal* 353 provides a detailed discussion of the legislation that will be useful reading in preparation for an essay question.

Chapter Summary:
Putting it all together

TEST YOURSELF

☐ Can you tick all the points from the revision checklist at the beginning of this chapter?

☐ Take the **end-of-chapter quiz** on the Companion Website.

☐ Test your knowledge of the cases below with the **revision flashcards** on the website.

☐ Attempt the essay question from the beginning of the chapter using the guidelines below.

☐ Go to the Companion Website to try out other questions.

Answer guidelines

See the essay question at the start of the chapter.

Points to remember when answering this question:

■ You should provide a brief description of the doctrine of privity, explaining that the doctrine derives from *Tweddle* v. *Atkinson, Dunlop* v. *Selfridge.*

■ You could then go on to discuss criticisms of this aspect of the doctrine (*Beswick* v. *Beswick, Woodar* v. *Wimpey, Darlington* v. *Wiltshier*).

■ Note how courts have developed exceptions (*Jackson* v. *Horizon Holidays*).

■ Note briefly that a number of statutory exceptions exist.

■ Explain that the Contracts (Rights of Third Parties) Act 1999 has reformed the doctrine of privity.

■ Explain that the two main provisions of the Act apply to most contracts. The parties to the contract can give rights to third parties in two ways (section 1): (1) contract expressly provides that the third party may enforce the term; (2) where the term of the contract purports to confer a benefit on the third party.

■ Explain why the second limb is more problematic – difficulties in interpretation (but note *Nisshin Shipping*); where more than one term for benefit of the third party *each term* will have to satisfy test.

Make your answer really stand out:

■ When using *Tweddle* to illustrate the fact that a third party cannot enforce a promise made for his benefit you could also link this to the point that the contract would fail for lack of consideration (see Chapter 2).

■ A good answer would also refer to the Law Commission's criticisms of the doctrine as well as the judicial criticism in case law.

■ When considering exceptions, the more relevant case examples you include, the better supported your answer will be (*Linden Gardens Trust, Darlington* v. *Wiltshier, Alfred McAlpine Construction Ltd* v. *Panatown*).

■ You could demonstrate your depth of understanding by briefly referring to agency, assignment and trusts as means of avoiding the doctrine.

■ In relation to the Contracts (Rights of Third Parties) Act 1999 a good answer would note that the third party does not become a party to the contract, that the parties to the contract may expressly state that the Act does not apply in whole or part to the contract, and that the parties to the contract may vary and rescind the third party's rights but only with the third party's consent in three situations.

■ A very good answer would briefly consider how past cases might be decided now: look at *Tweddle* v. *Atkinson, Beswick* v. *Beswick*. Note also *Dunlop* v. *Selfridge* where the contractual burden still cannot be imposed.

4
Contractual terms

A printable version of this topic map is available from www.pearsoned.co.uk/lawexpress

Revision Checklist

What you need to know:

- [ ] The distinction between a representation and a term of the contract and the consequences of the distinction
- [ ] The difference between express and implied contract terms
- [ ] The way in which terms are implied into a contract under common law
- [ ] The operation of statutory implied terms.

Introduction:
Contractual terms

Contracts are made up of contractual terms.

While the majority of these are expressly agreed by the parties entering into the contract, contracts may also include terms which are not expressly stated, but which are implied to give effect to the intention of the parties, or implied by custom or by law.

This chapter will begin by looking at the different types of pre-contractual statements, the means by which they may be incorporated into the contract and an indication of the remedies which may be available in the event of their breach. It will then move on to consider the classification of contractual terms into conditions, warranties and innominate terms and examine each of these in terms of their relative importance and the consequent action that may be taken if they are breached. Finally the chapter will look at the role of implied terms, with particular reference to the terms implied into consumer contracts by statute.

Essay question advice

Essay questions on contractual terms could concentrate on one area of the topic in particular or a much broader-ranging discussion of the means by which terms are incorporated into contracts. Such essay questions would tend to be unpopular with students as the operation of contractual terms is often either overlooked in selective revision or skimmed just in case the topic comes up as part of a problem question. This means that if you are equipped with a good understanding of contractual terms then you would be well placed for your answer to stand out from those done by students who are attempting the question as a last resort. Remember that unpopular questions tend to be done either very well, or very badly.

Sample question

Could you answer this question? Below is a typical essay question that could arise on this topic. Guidelines on answering the question are included at the end of the chapter, whilst a sample problem question and guidance on tackling it can be found on the Companion Website.

Essay question

The contents of a contract are not always written within it.
   Discuss.

◼ Representations and terms

Before a contract is formed, the parties will make various statements in the course of negotiation. Since these statements may form part of the contract, it is important to be able to distinguish between contractual terms and other statements. We must consider so-called 'puffs', representations and terms.

KEY DEFINITIONS

A **'puff'** is a boastful statement made in advertising.

A **representation** is a statement which induces a party to enter into a contract (but does not form part of it).

A **term** is a promise or undertaking which becomes part of the contract itself.

The distinction between these three types of statement is important as the legal consequences that result if a pre-contractual statement is false differs depending on the classification of the statement. This is so even though both representations and terms induced the formation of the contract. See Figure 4.1.

Figure 4.1

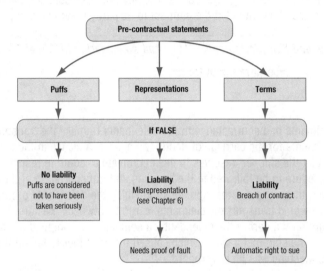

Incorporation of express terms

Given the distinction between the different types of pre-contractual statement, it follows that not all representations end up as terms of the contract. The distinction between representations and terms is generally decided by considering key questions:

▮ What was the intention of the parties?
▮ Were the statements intended to raise expectations which the contract should uphold?

The question put forward by the House of Lords in *Heilbut, Symons & Co.* v. *Buckleton* (1913) was as follows:

▮ Was there evidence of an intention by one or both parties that there should be a contractual liability in respect of the accuracy of the statement?

In order to answer these questions, there are a number of tests which the courts have developed.

Contract is in writing

If the contract is in writing, then the statements within it are usually regarded as terms rather than representations. It follows that statements which were made before the contract are considered to be mere representations (otherwise the parties would have reduced them to writing). The courts will, however, still consider the intention of the parties, in case they intended the contract to be partly in writing and partly oral.

KEY CASE

J Evans and Son (Portsmouth) Ltd v. *Andrea Mezario Ltd* [1976] 1 WLR 1078

Concerning: incorporation of terms

Facts

The claimants had contracted with the defendants to make the transport arrangements for the carriage of goods to England. A clause in the contract stated that the shipper 'reserves to itself complete freedom in respect of . . . the procedure to be followed in the handling and transportation of the goods.' However, there was a verbal agreement in which the defendants promised that they would transport the claimants' cargo below deck. Because of an oversight on the part of the defendants, a container was shipped to England on deck. The ship met a swell which caused the container to fall off the deck and the machine was lost overboard.

The claimants claimed damages against the defendants for the loss of the machine, alleging that the carriage of the container on deck had been a breach of the contract of carriage.

Legal principle

The court held that the oral promise was incorporated in the contract. Per Roskill LJ, the contract was partly oral, partly written and partly by conduct and in those circumstances the court was entitled to look at all the evidence to determine the bargain struck between the parties. It followed that the defendants were liable for breach of the oral promise.

Contract is signed

Where a written agreement is signed, the parties to it are considered to be in agreement with everything it contains *even if they have not read it.*

KEY CASE

L'Estrange v. *Graucob* [1934] 2 KB 394

Concerning: incorporation of terms; signed contract

Facts

Mrs L'Estrange owned a café. She ordered a cigarette machine from the manufacturers which was faulty. The contract, which she had signed, contained a clause stating that 'any express or implied condition, statement or warranty, statutory or otherwise not stated herein is hereby excluded'. L'Estrange claimed for breach of a term implied by the Sale of Goods Act 1893 that the goods were unfit for purpose. She also claimed that she had not seen the clause and therefore had no knowledge of its contents.

Legal principle

L'Estrange's claim failed. Scrutton LJ stated that:

'When a document containing contractual terms is signed, then, in the absence of fraud, or, I will add, misrepresentation, the party signing it is bound and it is wholly immaterial whether he has read the document or not.'

REVISION NOTE

Note that exclusions of liability for the terms implied by the Sale of Goods Act 1893 were allowed. This is not the case under the 1979 Act. These terms would also now be governed by the Unfair Contract Terms Act 1977 and the Unfair Terms in Consumer Contracts Regulations 1999. See Chapter 5.

The importance of the statement

The greater the importance attached to a particular statement by one party, the more likely it is to be considered to be a term. Therefore, if the party would not have entered into the contract if the statement had not been made, then that statement is highly likely to be considered a term – otherwise the contract would not be giving effect to the intention of the parties.

KEY CASE

Bannerman v. *White* (1861) 10 CBNS 844

Concerning: incorporation of terms; importance of statement

Facts

The defendant was the purchaser of hops. Before the contract was formed the purchaser stated that 'if they have been treated with sulphur, I am not

▶

71

KEY CASE

interested in even knowing the price of them'. The seller stated (wrongly) that they had not been so treated. When the purchaser discovered this, he repudiated the contract. The seller sued on the basis that the discussions were preliminary to the contract and not part of it.

Legal principle

The seller failed. The court held that the statement was so important to the purchaser that it became a term of the contract that had been breached.

This principle has also applied to an assurance that:

■ a new house would be 'as good as the show house' (*Birch* v. *Paramount Estates (Liverpool) Ltd* (1956)); and

■ a heifer (a young female cow) had not been used for breeding (*Couchman* v. *Hill* (1947)).

Reliance on specialist knowledge and skill

Where one party relies on a statement made with the specialist knowledge or skill of the other party in deciding whether or not to enter into a contract, then the statement may be considered to be a term of the contract.

KEY CASE

Dick Bentley Productions Ltd v. *Harold Smith (Motors) Ltd* [1965] 1 WLR 623

Concerning: incorporation of terms; specialist knowledge

Facts

The claimant asked the defendants to source a 'well vetted' Bentley. The defendants claimed that a particular car had done 20,000 miles since being fitted with a new engine and gearbox. It had, in fact, done 100,000 miles, which the claimant discovered after purchasing the car.

Legal principle

The statement regarding mileage was held to be a term of the contract. The claimant had relied on the specialist knowledge of the dealer in making the statement which was a major factor in his decision to enter into the contract.

However, in a similar case where an erroneous (but honest) statement as to a vehicle's age was made by a private seller with no expertise or specialist skill, the statement was not considered to be a term of the contract (*Oscar Chess Ltd* v. *Williams* (1957) but a representation: the party to whom the statement was made was a car dealer and was therefore perfectly capable of determining the veracity of the statement for themselves.

The timing of the statement

Where there is a significant lapse in time between the statement made and the formation of the contract, the courts are more likely to consider the statement as a representation rather than as a term of the contract.

KEY CASE

Routledge v. *McKay* [1954] 1 WLR 615

Concerning: incorporation of terms; lapse of time

Facts

A motorcycle was first registered in 1939. A new registration document was issued which erroneously stated this as 1941. In 1949 the then owner who was unaware of this inaccuracy stated that the age of the motorcycle was 1941 to a prospective buyer. The buyer bought the motorcycle a week later by written contract that did not stipulate the age of the motorcycle. He later discovered the true age and sued for breach of a term.

Legal principle

The buyer's claim failed. The court considered that the lapse of time was too great to infer that the contract was formed based on the statement of age and as such the statement was not incorporated as a term of the contract.

This view was also considered more recently in *Inntrepreneur Pub Co.* v. *East Crown Ltd* (2000) in which it was stated that the longer the interval between the statement and the contract, 'the greater the presumption that the parties did not intend the statement to have contractual effect'.

The parol evidence rule

The general 'parol evidence' rule states that where a contract has been reduced to writing, extrinsic evidence (whether written or oral) is inadmissible to add to, vary, or contradict its terms. In other words, at common law, a written contract is presumed to contain everything upon which the parties agreed and anything that is not embodied in the contract is considered never to have been intended to be included. This is so even if there is oral or written matter (such as earlier drafts of the contract or accompanying correspondence) which suggests otherwise.

The Law Commission (1976) recommended that the rule should be abolished, but by 1986 concluded that it did not stop the courts accepting parol evidence if this was consistent with the intention of the parties.

A number of exceptions to the basic rule have been developed:

■ If the written agreement was not intended to be the whole contract on which the parties had actually agreed, parol evidence is admissible (*J. Evans and Son (Portsmouth) Ltd* v. *Andrea Mezario Ltd* (1976)).
■ Parol evidence may be given to determine the validity of the contract.
■ Parol evidence can be used to show that the contract does not yet operate, or that it has ceased to operate (*Pym* v. *Campbell* (1856)).
■ Parol evidence can be used to show in what capacities the parties contracted (*Humfrey* v. *Dale* (1857)).
■ Parol evidence can be used to explain words or phrases which are ambiguous, or which, if taken literally, make no sense.
■ Parol evidence of custom is admissible 'to annex incidents to written contracts in matters with respect to which they are silent' (*Hutton* v. *Warren* (1836)).
■ Parol evidence may be used to show that the written document does not record the true agreement accurately, enabling the equitable remedy of rectification (*Webster* v. *Cecil* (1861)).
■ Parol evidence can be used to show that the parties made two related contracts, one written and the other oral (i.e. a collateral contract) (*City & Westminster Properties* v. *Mudd* (1959)).

■ Classification of terms

Terms which are incorporated into a contract fall into three categories:

■ conditions
■ warranties
■ innominate terms.

The distinction between these three types relates to their relative importance and the consequent action that can be taken in the event of their breach (see Figure 4.2).

Figure 4.2

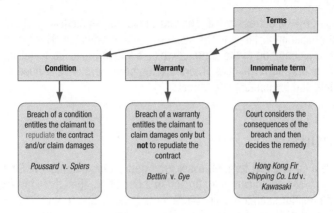

Conditions

A **condition** is said to 'go to the root' of the contract. Therefore conditions are the most important terms of the contract. It follows that the breach of a condition would mean that something essential to the contract had failed and as such the contract could not feasibly continue.

Breach of a condition allows the claimant to access the full range of contractual remedies.

REVISION NOTE

Remedies are covered in Chapter 9.

The injured claimant can sue for damages as well as repudiating his own obligations under the contract. In other words, the claimant can consider that his contractual obligations have ceased. Once discharged he is free from the contract.

KEY CASE

***Poussard* v. *Spiers and Pond* (1876) 1 QBD 410**

Concerning: breach of condition

Facts

An actress was under contract to appear as the lead in an operetta. She was taken ill and unable to attend the first performances. Her role was given to her understudy. Once recovered, she sued for breach of contract.

> **KEY CASE**
>
> **Legal principle**
>
> The claim by the actress failed. The court held that as the lead performer she was of crucial importance to the success of the production. This was therefore a condition of the contract which she had breached by failing to attend the first performances. Therefore the producers were entitled to repudiate and terminate the contract.

Warranties

A **warranty** is a contractual term of lesser importance than a condition. Since breach of a warranty is less significant than breach of a condition, then the contract might be able to continue after such a breach. Since a warranty does not 'go to the root' of a contract its breach is less likely to be fatal to the contract as a whole.

Therefore the remedies available to a claimant who has suffered a breach of warranty are limited to damages only. The injured party does not have the same right to repudiate the contract and consider themselves discharged from it in the same way as they would for breach of a condition.

> **KEY CASE**
>
> ***Bettini* v. *Gye* (1876) 1 QBD 183**
>
> **Concerning: breach of warranty**
>
> **Facts**
>
> The facts of this case are similar to those of *Poussard* v. *Spiers*. Here, a singer was under contract to appear in a series of concerts in different theatres. The contract included a term that he should attend rehearsals for six days before the live performances commenced. The singer did not attend the first three rehearsals. He was replaced. The singer sued for breach of contract.
>
> **Legal principle**
>
> The claim by the singer was successful. The court held that attendance at rehearsals was peripheral to the main purpose of the contract. Therefore the term was considered to be a warranty which entitled the producers to sue for damages but not to repudiate and terminate the contract by replacing the singer with another.

Just because a term is described in a contract as a condition does not mean that it is automatically a condition if its actual content is ancillary to the main purpose of the contract. It is the importance of the term that determines its classification, not the label that has been attached to it within the contract itself (*L. Schuler AG* v. *Wickman Machine Tool Sales* (1974)).

Innominate terms

The classification of contractual terms as conditions or warranties is based upon a determination as to whether the parties to the contract intended the term in question to be classified as one or the other.

More recently, the courts have developed an approach involving so-called '**innominate**' **terms**. This is a 'wait and see' approach: in other words, the courts look at the effects of the breach on the injured party to determine whether the breach itself was of a condition or a warranty. Therefore innominate terms are those whose classification is only determined once the effects of its breach are known. This gives the courts some flexibility in determining the appropriate remedy (repudiation and/or damages or damages only) which is fair to both parties.

KEY CASE

Hong Kong Fir Shipping Co. Ltd v. *Kawasaki Kisen Kaisha Ltd* [1962] 2 QB 26

Concerning: innominate terms

Facts

Kawasaki contracted with Hong Kong Fir Shipping to charter a vessel for a period of two years. A term in the contract required that the vessel was 'fitted in every way for ordinary cargo service' and that the owners would 'maintain her in a thoroughly efficient state ... during service'. Soon after beginning the voyage the ship broke down due to the incompetence of its engine room staff and, in any event, it was discovered that it was not seaworthy and in need of many repairs.

As a result the claimants were deprived of the use of the ship for 18 weeks while it was repaired to a seaworthy state. Kawasaki wrote to the owners repudiating the charter. Hong Kong Fir brought an action for wrongful repudiation, claiming that the term was only a warranty and not a condition.

Legal principle

It was held that Hong Kong Fir was in breach of the contract to deliver a seaworthy vessel, and also that it failed to maintain the vessel in an efficient state. However, this breach was not substantial enough to entitle the charterer to repudiation of the contract.

Lord Diplock stated that:

'There are ... many contractual undertakings of a more complex character which cannot be categorised as being 'conditions' or 'warranties' ... Of

▶

such undertakings all that can be predicated is that some breaches will and others will not give rise to an event which will deprive the party not in default of substantially the whole benefit which it was intended that he should obtain from the contract; and the legal consequences of a breach of such an undertaking, unless provided for expressly in the contract, depend upon the nature of the event to which the breach gives rise and do not follow automatically from a prior classification of the undertaking as a 'condition' or a 'warranty'.'

Despite the fact that the use of innominate terms can leave a contractual relationship on a footing of some uncertainty the approach taken in *Hong Kong Fir Shipping* has also been applied in later cases (*Cehave NV* v. *Bremer Handelsgesellschaft mbH (The Hansa Nord)* (1976)). However, notwithstanding the introduction of innominate terms, the court will still classify a term as a condition (irrespective of the consequences of the breach) if it considers that the circumstances merit doing so (*Bunge Corporation* v. *Tradax Export SA* (1981)).

Implied terms

As well as express terms which are part of the contract, certain terms can be implied into contracts in three ways:

■ by the court
■ by custom
■ by statute (see Figure 4.3).

Figure 4.3

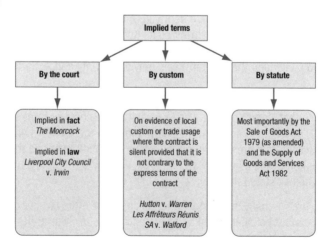

Terms implied by the court

The court may imply terms in *fact* or in *law*.

Terms implied in fact

A term will be implied in fact if it is obvious and necessary in order to give the contract business efficacy. The test used by the courts in this case is known as the *officious bystander* test, which was stated by MacKinnon LJ in *Shirlaw* v. *Southern Foundries Ltd* (1940) who considered that:

> *'Prima facie* that which is left to be implied is something so obvious that it goes without saying; so that, if, while the parties were making their bargain, an officious bystander were to suggest some express provision for it in the agreement, they would testily suppress him with a common "oh, of course!"'

KEY CASE

The Moorcock (1889) 14 PD 64

Concerning: terms implied in fact

Facts

The claimant entered into a contract with the defendants to dock and unload cargo from his ship at their wharf on the Thames. The ship was grounded at the jetty at low tide and broke up on rocks. The claimant sued for the damage to his ship. The defendants claimed that there was no express term relating to the safety of the ship and, as such, they could not be liable for breach of contract.

Legal principle

The court held that there was an implied term in the contract that the ship would not be damaged. This term was necessary in order to give the contract business efficacy. Therefore the defendants were liable for breach of this implied term.

Terms implied in law

As well as terms which are implied by the courts in fact, there are also terms which are implied by the courts in law. The distinction between the two is as follows:

▎ Terms implied in fact are inserted to represent the obvious, but unexpressed, wishes of the parties to the particular contract in question.

▎ Terms implied in law are inserted into the contract *regardless* of the wishes of the parties: typically to regulate a particular sort of agreement and often to protect the interests of the weaker party.

Liverpool City Council v. *Irwin* [1976] 2 WLR 562

Concerning: terms implied in law

Facts

The condition of a council tower block deteriorated such that the stairs and lifts were in disrepair and internal rubbish chutes were blocked. Irwin alleged a breach on the part of the council of its implied covenant for their quiet enjoyment of the property.

Legal principle

The House of Lords held that it was an implied term of the lease that the landlord should take reasonable care to keep the common parts of the block in a reasonable state of repair. The term was clearly not implied in fact. The 'officious bystander' test was not satisfied. The implication was also not required to give business efficacy to the contract.

The implication arose because the relationship between the parties made it desirable to place an obligation on the landlord as to the maintenance of the common parts of the premises. This was done by the imposition of a legal duty even though no contractual term could be implied in fact.

Customary implied terms

Terms may also be implied into a contract by custom: that is in response to (parol) evidence of local custom or usage in matters which relate to the contract in question where the contract itself is silent on the matter (*Hutton* v. *Warren* (1836)). However, terms will not be implied by custom where they would be contrary to the express terms of the contract (and thus the express intention of the parties not to abide by local custom or usage) (*Les Affréteurs Réunis SA* v. *Walford* (1919)).

Statutory implied terms

Finally, certain terms are implied into contracts by statute, primarily to protect parties where there is inequality of bargaining strength. For example, there are various terms that are implied into contracts of employment. However, perhaps the most commonly encountered statutory implied terms are those relating to consumer contracts which are inserted by the Sale of Goods Act 1979 (as amended by the Sale and Supply of Goods Act 1994) and the Supply of Goods and Services Act 1982.

Section 2(1) of the Sale of Goods Act 1979 defines a contract for the sale of goods as 'a contract by which the seller transfers or agrees to transfer the property in goods to the buyer for a money consideration called the price'. The main provisions of the Act which apply to a contract for the sale of goods are as follows. Note that some of them only apply to goods sold in the course of a business (as opposed to a private sale):

Sale of Goods Act 1979 (as amended)	Effect
Section 12 – Title	In a contract for the sale of goods there is an implied condition on the part of the seller that in the case of a sale he has a right to sell the goods and in the case of an agreement to sell he will have such a right at the time when the property is to pass.
Section 13 – Sale by description	Where there is a contract for the sale of goods by description there is an implied term that the goods will correspond with the description. Where there is a sale by sample and description the bulk of the goods must correspond with both the sample and the description.
Section 14(2) – Quality	Where the seller sells goods *in the course of a business* there is an implied term that the goods supplied under the contract are of satisfactory quality
Section 14(2A) – Satisfactory quality	Goods are of satisfactory quality if they *meet the standard that a reasonable person would regard as satisfactory* taking account of any description, the price and all other relevant circumstances.

▶

Sale of Goods Act 1979 (as amended)	Effect
Section 14(2B) – Quality	The quality of goods includes their state and condition and includes: Fitness for all the purposes for which goods of the kind in question are commonly supplied – appearance and finish – freedom from minor defects – safety – durability (this is not an exhaustive list).
Section 14(2C) – Circumstances in which quality of goods is not unsatisfactory	The quality of goods is not unsatisfactory in respect of specific defects which are specifically drawn to the buyer's attention before the contract is made or, upon examination of the goods by the buyer before the contract, defects which that examination ought to reveal.
Section 14(3) – Fitness for purpose	Where the seller sells goods *in the course of a business* and the buyer expressly or by implication makes known to the seller any particular purpose, there is an implied term that the goods are reasonably fit for that purpose (whether or not that is a purpose for which such goods are commonly supplied) *except* where the buyer does not rely, or it is unreasonable for him to rely, on the skill or judgement of the seller.

There are similar terms implied into contracts for 'work and materials' under the Supply of Goods and Services Act 1982 relating to:

▌ title (section 2)
▌ description (section 3)
▌ satisfactory quality and fitness for purpose (section 4)
▌ sample (section 5)
▌ work (section 13) – the standard of workmanship required involves the exercise of 'reasonable care and skill'.

Chapter Summary:
Putting it all together

Answer guidelines

See the essay question at the start of the chapter.

Points to remember when answering this question:

■ This is a very broad question which gives you little clue as to the sorts of material that you should cover. As such, it is important to spend a few moments before you start writing your answer to gather your thoughts and to sketch out a rough outline or structure to your answer. This will help to give a reasonable flow to your answer and prevent you from rambling.

■ You could distinguish between puffs, representations and terms, explaining that puffs and representations may not be written down, and they do not form the contents of a contract; however, oral pre-contractual statements may become terms of the contract.

■ If the contract is in writing then pre-contractual statements are often treated as mere representations, although this is not always the case – courts will consider the intentions of the parties (*Evans* v. *Mezario*).

■ Pre-contractual statements are also incorporated if they are important to one party (*Bannerman* v. *White*).

■ Statements may also become terms if they are made from a position of specialist knowledge or skill (*Dick Bentley* v. *Harold Smith Motors* contrasted with *Oscar Chess* v. *Williams*).

■ Although the parol evidence rule suggests that extrinsic evidence is inadmissible, there are a number of exceptions (particularly in relation to collateral contracts – one written, one oral: *City & Westminster Properties* v. *Mudd*).

■ Explain the role of implied terms and their origins (by the court, in fact and in law, by custom and by statute – with examples drawn from the Sale of Goods Act 1979).

■ Finally, come to a conclusion which draws all the points together and refers back to the original statement. There are many situations in which the contents of a contract are not written within it.

Make your answer really stand out:

■ Many students would discuss only the role of implied terms in an essay such as this. Therefore your answer will be much stronger if you also consider the ways in which oral pre-contractual statements can become terms of the contract.

■ The use of cases and relevant statutory provisions is essential. Since this is a very broad question, it will most likely attract a lot of answers which are based on a superficial or 'common sense' understanding of the area (resulting from insufficient revision or choosing this question as a last resort) and which therefore contain very little (or no) legal authority. Illustrating your answer with examples will demonstrate a commendable depth of knowledge which should attract better marks.

5
Exclusion of liability

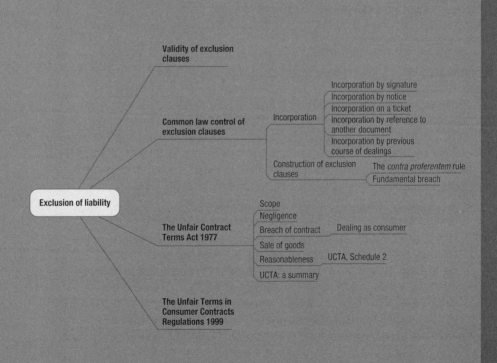

Validity of exclusion clauses

Common law control of exclusion clauses

Incorporation
- Incorporation by signature
- Incorporation by notice
- Incorporation on a ticket
- Incorporation by reference to another document
- Incorporation by previous course of dealings

Construction of exclusion clauses
- The *contra proferentem* rule
- Fundamental breach

The Unfair Contract Terms Act 1977
- Scope
- Negligence
- Breach of contract — Dealing as consumer
- Sale of goods
- Reasonableness — UCTA, Schedule 2
- UCTA: a summary

The Unfair Terms in Consumer Contracts Regulations 1999

Exclusion of liability

A printable version of this topic map is available from www.pearsoned.co.uk/lawexpress

Revision Checklist

What you need to know:

- [ ] The ways in which exclusion clauses may be incorporated into a contract
- [ ] The common law rules relating to the validity of exclusion clauses
- [ ] The statutory controls placed on the operation of exclusion clauses by the Unfair Contract Terms Act 1977 and the Unfair Terms in Consumer Contract Regulations 1999.

Introduction:
Exclusion of liability

Contract terms may attempt to exclude or limit one party's liability for breach, misrepresentation or negligence.

This chapter will consider the various ways in which exclusion clauses may be incorporated into contracts. It will examine the ways in which the common law has dealt with exclusion clauses and the increasing importance of legislative intervention in their control: most importantly via the Unfair Contract Terms Act 1977 and the Unfair Terms in Consumer Contract Regulations 1999. These operate primarily to protect consumers in situations which are considered to be 'unfair'.

Essay question advice

Essays on exclusion clauses could potentially concentrate on aspects of the statutory control of exclusion clauses, the common law position, or a comparison of both. As with all essay questions, it is important to have an extensive working knowledge of all aspects of the topic. Since this is a complicated area of law, it causes confusion amongst students so be sure that you can outline the basic requirements for the exclusion of liability with clarity and accuracy as this will give you an excellent foundation upon which to build your analysis.

Problem question advice

Problem questions on exclusion clauses will commonly include areas from other topics within contract law, particularly consumer law (Sale of Goods Act 1979) since there is a close relationship between UCTA and the Sale of Goods Act. Therefore it would be prudent not to revise exclusion clauses in isolation.

Sample question

Could you answer this question? Below is a typical problem question that could arise on this topic. Guidelines on answering the question are included at the end of the chapter, whilst a sample essay question and guidance on tackling it can be found on the Companion Website.

Problem question

Mark, who runs a minicab business, agreed to sell his second-hand car to Brian, a self-employed painter and decorator, for £5,000. This was a private arrangement. The sale agreement contained the following clauses:

'4. This vehicle is sold as seen with no undertaking about suitability or condition'.
'10. The seller accepts no liability in respect of any damage, harm or injury arising from the use of the vehicle for any reason whatsoever, including, for the avoidance of doubt, negligence on the part of the seller'.

Brian read the agreement before purchasing the car but did not sign it. That evening, while Brian was taking his wife, Kerry, out for a spin in his new car, the brakes jammed. Brian lost control and ran into a telegraph pole. As a result of the accident, Brian and Kerry were both injured. Brian suffered a whiplash injury to his back from the impact and was unable to work for six weeks. As a result he lost £5,000 in business. An engineer discovered that the brakes had been dangerously corroded for some time and could have failed at any moment.

(a) Advise Brian.
(b) Would your answer to (a) be any different if Mark had sold the car to Brian in the course of his business rather than as a private sale?

■Validity of exclusion clauses

There are a number of means by which the operation of exclusion clauses are controlled. Historically, a body of common law developed to govern their usage and more recently statute has intervened via the Unfair Contract Terms Act 1977 and the Unfair Terms in Consumer Contract Regulations 1999 (which give effect to EC Directive 93/13). In order to determine whether or not a particular clause is valid you should consider the common law position first, before applying each of the statutory controls in turn (see Figure 5.1).

Figure 5.1

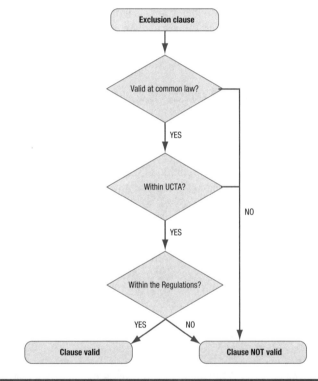

The Unfair Contract Terms Act 1977 is commonly referred to as 'UCTA'. We will refer to it as such in the rest of this chapter. Similarly, we will generally refer to the Unfair Terms in Consumer Contract Regulations 1999 as 'the Regulations'. If you do the same in the exam, to save you repeatedly having to write the lengthy names of the two pieces of legislation you should make sure that you refer to them by their full name the first time you refer to them in your answer and then abbreviate them thereafter. This will prove to the examiner that you do know the full names of the statutory controls (and their years).

Common law control of exclusion clauses

In order for an exclusion clause to be valid at common law it must satisfy three tests:

- it must be a term of the contract (that is, the clause must be incorporated in the contract); and
- it must cover the damage that was caused; and
- it must be reasonable.

Incorporation of exclusion clauses

The rules of incorporation of exclusion clauses are generally the same as those which apply to the incorporation of ordinary contractual terms.

Incorporation by signature

Where a document containing contractual terms is signed, then those terms are incorporated into the contract even if the party signing did not read it or understand it. Therefore, even if a party is unaware of, or does not understand, an exclusion clause, that exclusion clause will form part of the contract if the document has been signed.

> **KEY CASE**
>
> ***L'Estrange* v. *Graucob* [1934] 2 KB 394**
>
> **Concerning: incorporation of terms; signed contract**
>
> **Facts**
> The facts of this case are given in Chapter 4.
>
> **Legal principle**
> When a document containing contractual terms is signed, then, in the absence of fraud or misrepresentation, the party signing it is bound and it is wholly immaterial whether he has read the document or not.

Note, however, that a signed contract can be invalidated in whole or in part if there is a misrepresentation as to the effect of the exclusion clause:

KEY CASE

***Curtis* v. *Chemical Cleaning and Dyeing Co. Ltd* [1951] 1 KB 805**

Concerning: incorporation of terms; misrepresentation

Facts

The claimant took a wedding dress to be cleaned. She signed a document which contained a clause purporting to exempt the dry cleaners from liability for any damage 'howsoever caused'. When asked, the shop girl said that the clause only referred to exclusion for liability for damage to beads or sequins on the dress. The dress suffered bad staining and the claimant sued for damages. The dry cleaners attempted to rely on the exclusion clause.

Legal principle

The claim was successful. The court considered that the defendants could not rely on the exclusion clause because of the statement made by the assistant. The court said that the exclusion clause would be effective only in the event of damage to sequins or beads.

Incorporation by notice

The exclusion clause must be introduced *before* or *at the time* of the contract.

KEY CASE

***Olley* v. *Marlborough Court Hotel* [1949] 1 KB 532**

Concerning: exclusion clause; timing of notice; express notice

Facts

Mr and Mrs Olley booked into the Marlborough Court Hotel. The contract for their stay was formed at the point of check-in. While they were out for the evening, their key was taken from reception and used to gain access to their room. Mrs Olley's fur coat was stolen and she claimed damages from the hotel. The hotel attempted to disclaim liability based on a notice displayed on the wall of the Olley's hotel room which stated that:

'The proprietors will not hold themselves liable for articles lost or stolen unless handed to the manageress for safe custody.'

Legal principle

The court held that the hotel could not rely upon the exclusion clause to absolve themselves from liability. The contract was formed at the reception desk, at which time the Olleys had not been to their room and could not ▶

KEY CASE therefore have seen the notice. Therefore they were unaware of the clause at the time of the contract and, as such, it was not incorporated into the contract.

Not only must the term be introduced before or at the time of the contract, the courts require that the notice given of the exclusion clause must be *reasonable*. In other words, the party subject to the clause must be made sufficiently aware of its existence before or at the time that the contract was formed.

KEY CASE

Parker v. *South Eastern Railway Co.* (1877) 2 CPD 416

Concerning: incorporation of terms; reasonable notice

Facts

Mr Parker left luggage in the cloakroom at a railway station and was given a ticket in return for payment of a fee. The ticket had a clause on the back which provided that the railway company would not be liable in respect of any luggage exceeding £10 in value. Mr Parker's luggage was stolen. It was worth more than £10. The railway company attempted to exclude liability on the basis of the exclusion clause.

Legal principle

Mr Parker's claim was successful since the railway company could not prove that they had brought the claimant's attention to the exclusion clause. Therefore since the claimant had not been made sufficiently aware of the existence of the clause he was not bound by it.

Therefore the party who wishes to rely on an exclusion clause must take reasonable steps to bring it to the attention of the other party. However, what is reasonable is a question of objective fact. For instance in *Thompson* v. *LMS Railway Co.* (1930) it was noted that reasonable, *not actual* notice is required: therefore an illiterate railway passenger was considered to be bound by a clause since reasonably sufficient notice had been given to the ordinary railway traveller.

Incorporation on a ticket

Parker v. *South Eastern Railway* is an example of the so-called 'ticket cases' in which the courts consistently take the view that attention should be drawn to exclusion clauses by clear words.

Moreover, the clause will be incorporated only if it is on a document which might reasonably be considered to contain contractual terms.

Chapelton v. *Barry Urban District Council* [1940] 1 KB 532

Concerning: incorporation of terms; contractual document

Facts

The claimant hired two deckchairs and received two tickets from the council's beach attendant in return for payment. On the back of these tickets it was stated that 'The Council will not be liable for any accident or damage arising from the hire of the chair'. The claimant believed that the ticket was merely a receipt for payment and did not read it. One chair collapsed and the claimant was injured as a result. The claimant sued for damages; the council attempted to rely on the exclusion clause.

Legal principle

The claim was successful. The court did not accept that the exclusion clause had been incorporated into the contract since it had not been brought to the claimant's attention and held that it was unreasonable to assume that the ticket contained contractual terms.

In some instances the party seeking to rely on an exclusion clause has been required to go to great lengths to ensure that it has been brought to the attention of the other party. A very high degree of notice is required for such a clause to be effective:

Thornton v. *Shoe Lane Parking* [1971] 2 QB 163

Concerning: incorporation of terms; tickets; requirement of notice

Facts

There was a sign at the entrance to a car park which stated the parking fees and a notice that parking was 'at the owner's risk'. Drivers were required to stop at a barrier on entry to the car park and take a ticket from a machine. The barrier would then lift. Each ticket contained a statement saying that 'This ticket is issued subject to the conditions of issue as displayed on the premises'. The conditions of the contract were displayed on notices *inside* the car park. These included a clause which excluded liability for damage to property and personal injury. The claimant was injured in the car park and sued for damages. The defendants argued that they were covered by the exclusion clause.

▶

KEY CASE

Legal principle

The claim was successful. The court considered that the operators of the car park had not taken sufficient steps to draw the exclusion clause to the claimant's attention before the contract was made. Lord Denning concluded that the contract was formed *at the moment that the barrier was activated*:

'The customer has no chance of negotiating. He pays his money and gets a ticket. He cannot refuse it. He cannot get his money back. He may protest to the machine, even swear at it. But it will remain unmoved. He is committed beyond recall … The contract was concluded at that time.'

Incorporation by reference to another document

Where reference is made to an exemption clause in a document given to the claimant prior to the formation of the contract, the claimant's attention must still be drawn to the clause itself.

KEY CASE

Dillon v. *Baltic Shipping Co. Ltd (The Mikhail Lermontov)* **[1991] 2 Lloyd's Rep 155**

Concerning: incorporation of terms; reference to another document

Facts

The booking form for a cruise contained a clause that the contract of carriage was 'subject to conditions and regulations printed on the tickets'. The contract of carriage was issued some time after booking at the same time as the tickets. The ship sank and the claimant was injured. The shipping company attempted to rely on the exclusion clause.

Legal principle

The claim was successful. The court held that the booking form did not do enough to draw the claimant's attention to the exclusion clause; therefore it was not incorporated into the contract and the shipping company could not rely upon it.

This is also generally true for contracts which contain unusually burdensome contract terms. In *Interfoto Picture Library Ltd* v. *Stiletto Visual Programmes Ltd* (1988) Dillon LJ considered that 'if one condition in a set of printed conditions is particularly onerous or unusual, the party seeking to enforce it must show that that condition was fairly brought to the attention of the other party in the most explicit way'.

Incorporation by previous course of dealings

An exception to the general rule that there must be sufficient notice of the existence of an exclusion clause arises where there has been a previous course of dealing between the parties.

KEY CASE

J. Spurling Ltd v. *Bradshaw* [1956] 1 WLR 561

Concerning: incorporation of terms; previous course of dealings

Facts

The parties had contracted between each other for many years for the storage of goods in a warehouse. On one particular occasion the defendant delivered eight barrels of orange juice. A few days later the defendant received a document from the claimant which acknowledged receipt of the barrels. It also contained a clause purporting to exempt them from liability for loss or damage 'occasioned by the negligence, wrongful act or default' of themselves and their employees or agents. When the defendant collected the barrels some were empty, and some contained dirty water. He refused to pay the storage charge. The claimants sued.

Legal principle

Although the document containing the exclusion clause was not received until after the contract had been formed, the court held that the clause was incorporated into the contract as a result of a regular course of dealings between the parties over the years. Since the defendant had consistently received similar documents on previous occasions without complaint or renegotiation, he was bound by the terms contained therein.

This exception to the rule will apply only if the previous course of dealings has been consistent. In *McCutcheon* v. *David MacBrayne Ltd* (1964), the claimant had sometimes been asked to sign a 'risk note' containing an exclusion clause in relation to the use of a car ferry and sometimes not. Therefore, in a claim for damages after the claimant's car was written off as a result of the ferry sinking through the defendant's negligence, the court held that the exclusion clause could *not* be relied upon since there had not been a consistent course of dealings that would have allowed them to assume that the claimant knew of the existence of the clause. As such, the clause was held not to be incorporated within the contract.

In consumer contracts, where the exclusion clause seeks to protect the (stronger) position of the seller, the courts may require evidence of a large number of past transactions in order to find incorporation via a previous course of dealings (*Hollier* v. *Rambler Motors (AMC) Ltd* (1972)).

Construction of exclusion clauses

If it is established that an exclusion clause has been incorporated into the contract, it is then necessary to show that the clause covers the breach that has occurred. The contract as a whole will be considered. It is possible, therefore, that a validly incorporated exclusion clause may still fail.

The *contra proferentem* rule

The *contra proferentem* rule operates such that any ambiguity in the wording of a clause will be construed *against* the party that is attempting to rely upon it. In other words, in the event of any doubt in the wording of the clause, the benefit of that doubt will be given to the claimant.

KEY CASE

Houghton v. *Trafalgar Insurance Co. Ltd* [1953] 2 All ER 1409

Concerning: exclusion clause; *contra proferentem* rule

Facts

The claimant's motor insurance policy provided that the defendant insurers would not be liable if the vehicle carried an 'excess load'. The claimant had an accident while carrying six people in a five-seater car. The insurance company attempted to rely on the exclusion clause.

Legal principle

The claimant was successful. The Court of Appeal held that the term 'excess load' could mean either 'excess passengers' or 'excess weight' and interpreted it as meaning 'excess weight', using a narrow interpretation of 'load' as referring to goods and not to passengers.

If the exclusion clause attempts to exclude liability in negligence, then it must reach a very high standard of clarity and precision in drafting to be held to cover the breach that has occurred:

KEY CASE

Hollier v. *Rambler Motors (AMC) Ltd* [1972] QB 71

Concerning: exclusion clause; *contra proferentem* rule

Facts

Hollier had had a service or repair done by the defendant's garage on three of four occasions. It was the defendant's practice to use a form when

KEY CASE

undertaking a repair or service, and the defendant had used its form at least twice when dealing with Hollier. When used, the form was filled in to describe the details of work to be done and the price, and signed by Hollier. The form contained a term stating that 'the company is not responsible for damage caused by fire to customer's cars on the premises'.

While Hollier's car was in the garage, it was substantially damaged by a fire that arose from faulty electric wiring on the defendant's premises which had not been properly inspected or maintained. Hollier sued the defendant for damage to the car arising from its negligence. The defendant relied on the clause set out in the invoice.

Legal principle

The claimant was successful. The Court of Appeal held that the term was not incorporated into the contract by the previous course of dealings. In any case *obiter* the court considered that the clause did not protect the defendant. The clause was in general terms and did not refer specifically to negligence. For the garage to rely on the clause is must have stated clearly and unambiguously that it would not be liable in respect of its own negligence – otherwise a customer might reasonably conclude that the garage was not generally liable except for the situation in which the fire was caused by its own negligence.

Fundamental breach

Even where the clause does cover the breach, the courts developed a position where they tended not to allow an exclusion clause to protect a party from liability for a fundamental breach of contract. However, this doctrine of fundamental breach was ultimately rejected by the House of Lords:

KEY CASE

Photo Production Ltd v. Securicor Transport Ltd [1980] AC 827

Concerning: exclusion clause; fundamental breach

Facts

The claimants had contracted with Securicor on Securicor's standard terms to provide a night patrol to protect their factory. A clause in the standard terms provided that 'Under no circumstances shall the Company be responsible for any injurious act or default by any employee of the company unless such act or default could have been foreseen and avoided by the exercise of due diligence on the part of the Company as his employer'. One of the defendant's guards lit a fire inside the factory. This got out of control and destroyed the factory.

Legal principle

At first instance, the court held that the exclusion clause did cover the breach. On appeal, the Court of Appeal applied the doctrine of fundamental breach, reasoning that the breach was so serious that it effectively breached the whole contract and thus the exclusion clause did not apply. However, the House of Lords reversed the decision of the Court of Appeal: although the defendants were in breach, they were allowed to rely on the exclusion clause since it clearly and unambiguously covered the breach that had occurred.

■ The Unfair Contract Terms Act 1977

Although the common law has traditionally been used to control the operation of exclusion clauses, the most effective control is now found within legislation. The Unfair Contract Terms Act 1977 ('UCTA') seeks to impose statutory limits on the extent to which civil liability for breach of contract, for negligence or other breach of duty can be avoided by means of contract terms.

Scope

UCTA generally applies to 'business liability'. This is defined in section 1(3) as liability for breach of obligations or duties arising:

(a) from things done or to be done by a person in the course of a business (whether his own business or another's); or
(b) from the occupation of premises used for business purposes of the occupier.

Therefore, private transactions (that is non-business agreements between two private individuals) are *not* covered by UCTA.

The exceptions to this are:

■ implied terms in sale of goods and hire-purchase contracts (UCTA, section 6);
■ implied terms in supply of goods and services contracts (UCTA, section 7);
■ misrepresentation (UCTA, section 8).

The Act does not extend to certain kinds of contracts. These are listed in Schedule 1 and include:

■ any contract of insurance;
■ any contract relating to the creation, transfer or termination of an interest in land;
■ any contract so far as it relates to the creation, transfer or termination of a right or interest in any patent, trade mark, copyright or design right, registered design, technical or commercial information or other intellectual property.

Negligence

Section 2(1) of UCTA provides that liability for death or personal injury resulting from negligence cannot be excluded by reference to any contract term or notice.

Section 2(2) of UCTA provides that for loss or damage other than death or personal injury, liability may be excluded or limited so far as the term satisfies the reasonableness test (see below).

Breach of contract

Section 3(2)(a) of UCTA provides that where one party 'deals as consumer' or deals on the other's written standard terms of business, then the other party cannot exclude or restrict liability for breach of contract, unless the term satisfies the reasonableness test (see below).

Dealing as consumer

For the purposes of UCTA, 'dealing as consumer' is defined in section 12(1). In order to deal as consumer:

■ one party must not make the contract in the course of a business nor hold himself out as doing so; and
■ the other party must make the contract in the course of a business;
■ in the case of a contract governed by the law of sale of goods or hire purchase, the goods to which the contract relates must be of a type ordinarily supplied for private use or consumption (unless the first party is an individual, in which case this requirement does not apply).

Section 12(2) of UCTA provides two examples of instances where a party specifically does not deal as consumer:

■ where the party is an individual and the goods are secondhand and sold at a private auction which has the opportunity for buyers to attend the sale in person;
■ where the party is not an individual and the goods are sold by auction or competitive tender.

Note, therefore, that a 'consumer' can be a natural person or a legal person (a company). In *R & B Customs Brokers Co. Ltd* v. *United Dominions Trust Ltd* (1988), the claimant company, which was a shipping agency, bought a car for a director to be used for business and private use. It had bought cars once or twice before. The sale was arranged by the defendant finance company. The contract excluded the implied conditions about merchantable quality. The car leaked badly. It was held by the Court of Appeal that where a transaction was only incidental to a business activity, a degree of regularity was required before a transaction could be said to be an integral part of the business carried on and so entered into in the course of that business. Since here the car was only the second or third vehicle acquired by the claimants, there was not a sufficient degree of regularity capable of establishing that the contract was anything more than part of a consumer transaction. Therefore, this was a consumer sale. This approach was also followed in *Feldaroll Foundry plc* v. *Hermes Leasing (London) Ltd* (2004).

Finally, UCTA section 12(3), provides that the burden falls on the party seeking to rely on the exclusion clause to disprove that the contract is a consumer contract.

Sale of goods

REVISION NOTE

There are several terms implied into contracts for the sale of goods and the supply of goods and services. These were covered in Chapter 4. Before continuing with your revision of UCTA, it would be useful to review the operation of these implied terms.

Where the contract is for the sale of goods, there are a number of terms which are implied into the contract by the Sale of Goods Act 1979 (SGA 1979).

Section 6(1) of UCTA provides that liability for breach of section 12 of SGA 1979 (that is, the implied condition relating to title) cannot be excluded.

Section 6(2) of UCTA provides that *provided that the claimant is dealing as consumer* liability for breaches of the implied conditions as to:

■ conformity with description (SGA 1979, section 13)
■ quality or fitness (SGA 1979, section 14)
■ conformity with sample (SGA 1979, section 15)

cannot be excluded. Here, 'dealing as consumer' has the same meaning as in the discussion of breach of contract above.

If a person is not dealing as consumer, then liability can be excluded for breach of the implied terms but only in so far as the term satisfies the requirements of reasonableness (UCTA, section 6(3)).

There are similar provisions in UCTA, section 7 which relate to the terms implied into contracts for the supply of goods and services by the Supply of Goods and Services Act 1982 ('SGSA 1982'). These apply to contract terms excluding or restricting liability for breach of an 'implied obligation' in a contract under which the possession or ownership of goods passes but which are *not* contracts for the sale of goods. Again, the implied condition as to title (SGSA 1982, section 2) can never be excluded. *Provided that the claimant is dealing as consumer* liability for breaches of the implied conditions as to:

5 EXCLUSION OF LIABILITY

- transfer by description (SGSA 1982, section 3)
- quality or fitness (SGSA 1982, section 4)
- transfer by sample (SGSA 1982, section 5)

cannot be excluded. Where a person is not dealing as consumer, then liability can be excluded for breach of the implied terms but only in so far as the term satisfies the requirements of reasonableness UCTA, section 7(3)).

Reasonableness

The test for reasonableness in UCTA is found in section 11. It applies to the following sections:

- section 2(2): relating to exclusion of liability for loss other than death or personal injury caused by negligence;
- section 3: relating to liability for breach of contract, substantially different performance or no performance, where one party deals as consumer or deals on the other's standard form contract;
- section 4: relating to liability for indemnity;
- section 6(3): relating to breaches of the implied conditions in sections 13, 14(2), and (3) and 15 of the Sale of Goods Act 1979 for non-consumer contracts;
- section 7(3): relating to breaches of the implied conditions in sections 3, 4 and 5 of the Supply of Goods and Services Act 1982;
- section 8: relating to exclusions for misrepresentation.

KEY STATUTE

Unfair Contract Terms Act 1977, section 11

'(1) In relation to a contract term, the requirement of reasonableness ... is that the term shall have been a fair and reasonable one to be included having regard to the circumstances which were, or ought reasonably to have been, known to or in the contemplation of the parties when the contract was made.

(2) In determining for the purposes of section 6 or 7 [UCTA] above whether a contract term satisfies the requirement of reasonableness, regard shall be had in particular to the matters specified in Schedule 2 to this Act ...

(3) In relation to a notice (not ... having contractual effect), the requirement of reasonableness under this Act is that it should be fair and reasonable to allow reliance on it, having regard to all the circumstances obtaining when the liability arose or (but for the notice) would have arisen.

(4) Where by reference to a contract term or notice a person seeks to restrict liability to a specified sum of money, and the question arises ... whether the term or notice satisfies the requirement of reasonableness, regard shall be had in particular ... to –

▶

> (a) the resources which he could expect to be available to him for the purpose of meeting the liability should it arise; and
> (b) how far it was open to him to cover himself by insurance.
> (5) It is for those claiming that a contract term or notice satisfies the requirement of reasonableness to show that it does.'

FURTHER THINKING

Section 11(1) provides when the reasonableness test is to be applied – the key point here is that it must have been reasonable in all the circumstances *when the contract was made*. In the case of clauses which attempt to limit liability, then by section 11(4) the court must consider the resources that the defendant has available to meet that liability and whether the defendant had the possibility to protect himself by insurance. Section 11(5) establishes that the burden of proof to establish reasonableness of a contract term is on the defendant – in other words, the party which is attempting to rely upon the exclusion clause has to prove that it is reasonable within the meaning of section 11(1) (*Warren* v. *Truprint Ltd* (1986)). It is important that you are able to appreciate these points to ensure that you apply the law correctly.

UCTA Schedule 2

Section 11(2) of UCTA refers to Schedule 2 to the Act, which provides guidelines of the application of the reasonableness test. The criteria which should be considered are as follows:

■ the strength of the bargaining positions of the parties relative to each other;
■ whether the customer received an inducement to agree to the term (*R.W. Green Ltd* v. *Cade Bros Farms* (1978));
■ whether the customer knew or ought reasonably to have known of the existence and the extent of the term (having regard, among other things, to any trade custom and any previous course of dealing between the parties);
■ where the term excludes or restricts any relevant liability if some condition was not complied with, whether it was reasonable at the time of the contract to expect that compliance with that condition would be practicable;
■ whether the goods were manufactured, processed or adapted to the special order of the customer.

Examples of the application of the reasonableness test can be found in *George Mitchell (Chesterhall) Ltd* v. *Finney Lock Seeds* (1983), *Smith* v. *Eric S. Bush* (1990) and *Watford Electronics Ltd* v. *Sanderson CFL Ltd* (2001).

UCTA: A summary

Source of liability	Effect on consumer	Effect on non-consumer
Negligence leading to death or injury	Void: UCTA, s 2(1)	Void: UCTA, s 2(1)
Negligence leading to other loss or damage	Acceptable if reasonable: UCTA, s 2(1)	Acceptable if reasonable: UCTA, s 2(1)
Breach of standard-form contract	Acceptable if reasonable: UCTA, s 3(2)(a)	UCTA does not apply
Sale of goods with defective title (SGA 1979, s 12)	Void: UCTA, s 6(1)	Void: UCTA, s 6(1)
Sale of goods that do not match their description (SGA 1979, s 13)	Void: UCTA, s 6(2)	Acceptable if reasonable: UCTA, s 6(3)
Sale of goods that are of unsatisfactory quality (SGA 1979, s 14)	Void: UCTA, s 6(2)	Acceptable if reasonable: UCTA, s 6(3)
Sale of goods that do not match their sample (SGA 1979, s 15)	Void: UCTA, s 6(2)	Acceptable if reasonable: UCTA, s 6(3)
Supply of goods and services: defective title (SGSA 1982, s 3)	Void: UCTA, s 7(3A)	Void: UCTA, s 7(3A)
Supply of goods and services: goods do not match description (SGSA 1982, s 3)	Void: UCTA, s 7(2)	Acceptable if reasonable: UCTA, s 7(3)
Supply of goods and services: goods of unsatisfactory quality or fitness (SGSA 1982, s 4)	Void: UCTA, s 7(2)	Acceptable if reasonable: UCTA, s 7(3)
Supply of goods and services: goods do not match sample (SGSA 1982, s 5)	Void: UCTA, s 7(2)	Acceptable if reasonable: UCTA, s 7(3)

▶

Source of liability	Effect on consumer	Effect on non-consumer
Misrepresentation (Misrepresentation Act 1967, s 3)	Acceptable if reasonable: UCTA, s 8(1)	Acceptable if reasonable: UCTA, s 8(1)

■ The Unfair Terms in Consumer Contract Regulations 1999

The Unfair Terms in Consumer Contract Regulations 1999 (SI 1999/2083) ('the Regulations') resulted from the EC Directive on Unfair Contract Terms in Consumer Contracts (93/13/EC) which required member states to ensure that 'adequate and effective means exist to prevent the continued use of unfair terms in contracts concluded with customers. In some respects the Regulations are narrower than UCTA, although they are wider in others:

Narrower than UCTA	Wider than UCTA
Regulations apply to only contracts between business and consumer (therefore they do not apply to contracts between businesses)	Apply to all types of contracts
	Consider the fairness of contracts as a whole and not just the fairness of exclusion clauses.

The main provisions of the Regulations are as follows:

Regulation	Effect
3(1) Definition of consumer	Defines a consumer as 'any *natural* person who … is acting for purposes which are outside his trade, business or profession'. Therefore this excludes companies, which are *artificial* legal persons (*Standard Bank London Ltd* v. *Apostolakis* (2001)).
4 Scope of the Regulations	Provides that the Regulations apply in relation to unfair terms in contracts concluded between a seller or a supplier and a consumer (as defined in Regulation 3(1)).

▶

Regulation	Effect
5(1) Unfair terms	Provides that a contractual term which has not been individually negotiated shall be regarded as unfair if, contrary to the requirement of good faith, it causes a *significant imbalance* in the parties' rights and obligations arising under the contract, *to the detriment of the consumer.*
5(2)	Defines a term which has not been individually negotiated as one which has been drafted in advance and the consumer has therefore not been able to influence the substance of the term.
6 Assessment of unfair terms	Provides that (in so far as a term is in plain intelligible language), the assessment of the fairness of a term shall not relate to the definition of the main subject matter of the contract, or to the adequacy of the price or remuneration, as against the goods or services supplied in exchange. In other words, the Regulations are not concerned with the fairness of core terms such as subject matter of the contract or the price paid.
7 Plain language; *contra proferentem* rule	Provides that any written term of a contract must be expressed in plain, intelligible language. Where there is doubt about the meaning of a written term, the interpretation which is most favourable to the consumer shall prevail. This has the same effect as the *contra proferentem* rule.
8 Consequences of unfairness	Unfair terms shall not be binding on the consumer. However, the contract will remain in existence if it can do so without the offensive term.
10 Supervision	Provides that the Director General of Fair Trading is the general supervisor of compliance with the Regulations. He is authorised to receive complaints about breaches (in other words, consumers may complain directly to him about unfair terms) and to apply for injunctions to restrain the use of unfair terms (*Director General of Fair Trading* v. *First National Bank* (2001)).

The Regulations also offer an indicative and non-exhaustive list of terms which may be regarded as unfair. Examples of these are terms which have the object or effect of:

∎ excluding or limiting the legal liability of a seller or supplier in the event of the death or personal injury of a consumer;
∎ inappropriately excluding or limiting the legal rights of the consumer in the event of total or partial non-performance or inadequate performance by the seller;

■ requiring any consumer who fails to fulfil his obligation to pay a disproportionately high sum in compensation;

■ enabling the seller or supplier to alter the terms of the contract unilaterally without a valid reason which is specified in the contract;

■ enabling the seller or supplier to alter unilaterally without a valid reason any characteristics of the product or service to be provided;

■ providing for the price of goods to be determined at the time of delivery or allowing a seller of goods or supplier of services to increase their price without in both cases giving the consumer the corresponding right to cancel the contract if the final price is too high in relation to the price agreed when the contract was concluded;

■ giving the seller or supplier the right to determine whether the goods or services supplied are in conformity with the contract.

Chapter Summary:
Putting it all together

TEST YOURSELF

☐ Can you tick all the points from the revision checklist at the beginning of this chapter?

☐ Take the **end-of-chapter quiz** on the Companion Website.

☐ Test your knowledge of the cases below with the **revision flashcards** on the website.

☐ Attempt the problem question from the beginning of the chapter using the guidelines below.

☐ Go to the Companion Website to try out other questions.

Answer guidelines

See the problem question at the start of the chapter.

Points to remember when answering this question:
■ For Brian to be successful, he must establish that the exclusion clauses are not valid.
■ In part (a) the key point is that the transaction is a private sale.
■ Does the fact that the car had defective brakes constitute breach of contract? Since the car is not sold in the course of a business then the terms relating to quality and fitness for purpose implied by section 14 of the Sale of Goods Act 1979 do not apply.

■ Are the exclusion clauses incorporated into the contract? They are contained in a written sales agreement at the time of sale – so yes (*Olley* v. *Marlborough Court Hotel*).

■ The fact that Brian did not sign the agreement is irrelevant (*L'Estrange* v. *Graucob*).

■ Do the clauses cover the defect and damage? Yes – the clauses refer to no undertaking about condition and no liability for harm or injury.

■ Even though this is a fundamental breach, an exclusion clause may still cover such a breach at common law (*Photo Production Ltd* v. *Securicor*).

■ The clauses are valid at common law.

■ Private transactions are not covered by UCTA or the Regulations.

■ *Therefore the clauses are valid and Brian has no claim against Mark.*

■ In part (b) the transaction is carried out in the course of a business. This will bring both the Sale of Goods Act 1979 and UCTA into consideration, even though the clauses would most likely survive the common law tests (as shown in part (a)).

■ Section 14 of SGA 1979 implies a condition that the goods must be of satisfactory condition – including fitness for purpose – it is unlikely that the car was fit for purpose at the time of sale (consider short space of time between purchase and failure and the findings of the engineer's report).

■ Section 1(3) of UCTA – the transaction was made in the course of a business, so UCTA will apply.

■ As against a business, the exclusion clause relating to breach of the term implied by section 14 of SGA 1979 will be acceptable if reasonable – UCTA, section 6(3).

■ You should consider the reasonableness test here: UCTA, section 11 plus Schedule 2 and *George Mitchell* v. *Finney Lock Seeds*.

■ It is up to Mark to show that the clauses are reasonable (UCTA, section 11(5)).

■ If Brian can establish that Mark was negligent in selling the car, then the exclusion clause will be invalid in any event since section 2(1) of UCTA will render any clause attempting to exclude liability for personal injury in negligence ineffective.

■ Therefore, the clause relating to the condition of the car will be subject to the reasonableness test (and will probably fail on being unreasonably broad).

■ The clause relating to liability for injury will automatically fail.

■ Brian is therefore likely to be successful and will be awarded damages (compensation).

Make your answer really stand out:

■ As well as stating the relevant law in relation to the contractual terms you are being asked to advise one of the parties. You should therefore remember to cover points such as who will have the burden of proof where points are arguable.

■ You should give an assessment as to the likely outcome of each claim – in terms of strength of case and remedy sought.

■ Be precise when considering the many statutory provisions that apply to this area: try to provide section numbers for the various parts of the Sale of Goods Act 1979 and UCTA.

■ Avoid a confused answer by dealing with each clause separately.

6
Misrepresentation, mistake and illegality

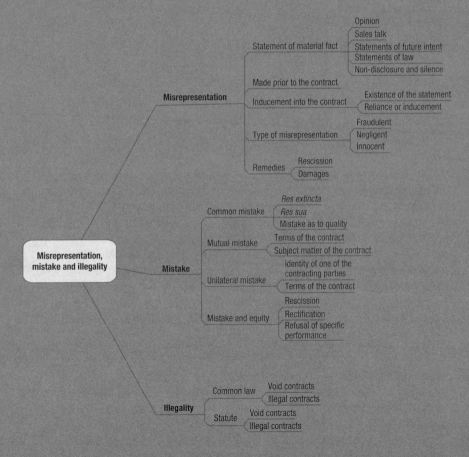

A printable version of this topic map is available from www.pearsoned.co.uk/lawexpress

Revision Checklist

What you need to know:

- [ ] The elements of misrepresentation
- [ ] The differences between fraudulent, negligent and innocent misrepresentation
- [ ] Remedies that may be available for misrepresentation
- [ ] The operation of common, mutual and unilateral mistake
- [ ] Remedies that may be available for mistake
- [ ] The principles of illegality in contract.

Introduction:
Misrepresentation, mistake and illegality

Misrepresentation, mistake and illegality are factors which invalidate otherwise valid contracts.

They are also known as 'vitiating factors'. Even though a contract may be formed perfectly validly in law (that is, the elements of a binding contract – offer, acceptance, consideration and intention to create legal relations are all present) the contract may still be unenforceable due to other factors. These factors are the sorts of things that, had they been known by both parties at the time of the contract being formed, then the parties might never have reached agreement and thus the contract might never have been formed. Depending on the particular circumstances, a contract may be **void** (treated as though it had never been valid at all) or **voidable** (avoided by one party; that is, it is not automatically void, but one of the parties may choose to treat it as void and thus unenforceable, or continue with it if they so desire, or amend its terms to those which are more preferable).

Essay question advice

There is plenty of case law on mistake, misrepresentation and illegality so there is immense scope for an essay question on these topics. Make sure that you have a firm foundation of knowledge that covers the basic elements of these areas of law as well as familiarity with the body of cases. Remember that an essay requires that you demonstrate your ability to engage in critical analysis so make note of any weaknesses in the law or differences of opinion between the courts on particular issues.

Problem question advice

Problem questions that include misrepresentation and/or mistake are common. Look out for facts that suggest that one party to the contract harboured an inaccurate belief about some fact associated with the performance of the contract as a clue that these topics are relevant. You should then consider whether this inaccurate belief arose due to some factor associated solely with the mistaken party (mistake) or was in some way planted in the mistaken party's mind by the other party (misrepresentation). Do not overlook revision of illegality although it arises in problem questions less frequently than mistake and misrepresentation.

Sample question

Could you answer this question? Below is a typical problem question that could arise on this topic. Guidelines on answering the question are included at the end of the chapter, whilst a sample essay question and guidance on tackling it can be found on the Companion Website.

Problem question

Rebecca owned a film studio. She negotiated with Thomas who owned a cinema regarding purchase of the rights to show a film for four weeks at £25,000. Rebecca said that the film was a real bargain and an extraordinary new visual experience since the film was the only one on the market to use 3D-HD photography; she also thought that the film could be shown on small screens as well as panoramic ones although she had never shown it on small screens herself. She pointed to a report on her desk containing the estimated average takings of the film when shown at the Odeon in Leicester Square. Thomas read the report. It stated that on average the film had made approximately £75,000 a week. He thought he might send his accountant around to look at the accounts to verify the report, but decided not to. He was impressed with what Rebecca had said and in any event, he wanted to be the first cinema in his town to show a 3D-HD film.

Thomas purchased the film. It turned out to be a disaster. The photography was ordinary. After the negotiations, but before the sale, three other films were released in London that had 3D-HD photography but Rebecca forgot to tell Thomas before Thomas bought the film. The film was not able to be shown on small screens. Thomas only made £7,000 per week over the four-week period. This was not surprising as the report had been prepared by Rebecca's trainee accountant Chris, who had got the figures wrong as he was having problems with his new laptop.

Had the mistake not been made, the report would have read £7,500 per week. Rebecca had not seen the film nor read the report before directing Thomas's attention to it. Chris has now left Rebecca's employment.

Advise Thomas whether he might have any remedy in contract against Rebecca.

■Misrepresentation

Before considering the elements of misrepresentation in detail, it is first necessary to define what is meant by an actionable misrepresentation.

KEY DEFINITION

An **actionable misrepresentation** is a statement of material fact made prior to the contract by one party to the contract to the other which is false or misleading and which induced the other party to enter into the contract.

You can see that there are a number of elements to a misrepresentation, which we will now explore in more detail.

A statement of material fact

There are certain statements which might not be treated as being statements of material fact:

- opinion
- mere sales talk
- statements of future intention or conduct
- statements of law.

It is also necessary to consider whether silence (or failure to disclose certain information) can ever amount to a misrepresentation.

Opinion

A false statement of opinion is not a misrepresentation as to fact.

KEY CASE

Bissett v. Wilkinson [1927] AC 177

Concerning: misrepresentation; statement of opinion

Facts

The claimant purchased two pieces of land from the defendant for the purpose of sheep farming. During negotiations the defendant said that he believed that it would be suitable for 2,000 sheep. The claimant therefore bought the land in that belief. Both parties knew that the defendant had not

---

▶

carried on sheep farming on the land. The land would not, in fact, hold 2,000 sheep.

Legal principle

The court upheld the decision of the trial judge who considered that:

> 'In ordinary circumstances, any statement made by an owner who has been occupying his own farm as to its carrying capacity would be regarded as a statement of fact. . . . This, however, is not such a case. . . . In these circumstances . . . the defendants were not justified in regarding anything said by the plaintiff [now claimant] as to the carrying capacity as being anything more than an expression of his opinion on the subject.'

Therefore a statement of opinion cannot give rise to an actionable misrepresentation. In the absence of fraud, the claimant had no basis on which to rescind the contract.

However, where the party making the statement has some special knowledge or skill which gives weight to their opinion, then their opinion may be treated as being an implied representation of fact, and therefore capable of being a misrepresentation (*Smith* v. *Land and House Property Corp* (1884)).

Sales talk

Mere 'sales talk' or 'puff' is not considered to be a statement of fact. The courts treat such utterances as idle boasts and attach no contractual significance to them.

KEY CASE

Dimmock v. *Hallett* (1866) 2 Ch App 21

Concerning: misrepresentation; sales talk

Facts

During negotiations for the sale of land, the land was described as 'fertile and improvable'.

Legal principle

The court considered that this statement had insufficient substance to be classed as a representation.

This was also considered in *Carlill* v. *Carbolic Smoke Ball Co. Ltd* (see Chapter 1).

Statements of future intent

Since a misrepresentation is a false representation of material fact, it follows that since a statement which expresses a future intention is speculation rather than fact, it cannot amount to a misrepresentation. However, in much the same way that an opinion can be treated as fact where the party has special knowledge, if the statement of future intention falsely represents the actual intention (in other words, it is a wilful lie) then it may also be treated as a misrepresentation of fact:

KEY CASE

Edgington v. *Fitzmaurice* (1885) 29 Ch D 459

Concerning: misrepresentation; statements of future intention

Facts
The claimant was a shareholder who received a circular issued by the directors of a company requesting loans to the amount of £25,000 with interest in order to grow their business. However, the money was in fact to be used to pay off the company's debt, not to grow the business. The claimant, who had taken debentures, claimed repayment of his money on the ground that it had been obtained from him by misrepresentation.

Legal principle
The court held that the untrue statement as to future intention was a misrepresentation of fact.

Statements of law

Traditionally, a false statement of law cannot amount to a misrepresentation because there is a presumption that everyone knows the law and therefore it cannot be falsely stated. However, since the distinction between fact and law is not always clear cut it can be difficult to distinguish between a statement of law and a statement of fact:

KEY CASE

Solle v. *Butcher* [1950] 1 KB 671

Concerning: statements of law

Facts
Before the Second World War, a house had been converted into flats. After the war, the defendant leased the building with the intention to repair bomb damage and undertake other improvements. The claimant and defendant discussed the rents to be charged after the work had been completed. The

▶

KEY CASE defendant stated that the flat had become a new and separate dwelling by reason of change of identity, and was therefore not subject to the Rent Restriction Acts.

Legal principle

This was held to be a statement of fact and therefore actionable.

However, following *Pankhania* v. *London Borough of Hackney* (2002), it seems that a misrepresentation of law *can* amount to an actionable misrepresentation. Here, the particulars of a commercial property for sale by auction described it as being sold subject to a 'licence' which was terminable on three months' notice. The court held that this 'licence' was actually a tenancy and therefore was protected under Part II of the Landlord and Tenant Act 1954. The buyer had entered into a contract to buy the property on the representation that National Car Parks Ltd had a licence that was terminable on three months' notice and was successful in his claim for damages as a result of misrepresentation. The court held that there had been a misrepresentation as to the legal character of the 'licence'.

Non-disclosure of information and silence

Generally, and perhaps unsurprisingly, silence cannot amount to a misrepresentation. In other words, there is no duty for a party who is about to enter into a contract to disclose material facts known to that party but not to the other party:

KEY CASE

Keates v. *Cadogan* (1851) 10 CB 591

Concerning: misrepresentation; silence

Facts

A landlord who was letting his house did not tell the tenant that it was in a ruinous condition.

Legal principle

This failure to disclose material information was held not to be a misrepresentation.

However, this is a general rule, and the courts may decide that in particular circumstances there is a positive duty of disclosure (for example, see *Sybron Corporation* v. *Rochem* (1984) which involved the 'covering up and deliberate concealing' of a defect).

The general rule is also subject to a number of established exceptions:

- contracts of utmost good faith (*uberrimae fidei*)
- where there has been a change in circumstances
- half-truths
- where there is a fiduciary relationship.

Contracts of utmost good faith (*uberrimae fidei*)

In contracts of utmost good faith there is a duty to disclose all material facts. These typically arise where one party is in a strong position to know the truth and the other is in a weak position. Examples of such contracts include:

- Contracts of insurance – these are the leading examples of contracts of utmost good faith. There is a duty on the insured party to disclose all material facts which are relevant to the insurer's acceptance of the risk and the insurance premium to be paid in respect of that risk. Insurance contracts are voidable if there has not been full disclosure of material facts.
- Contracts involving family arrangements – for instance, in agreements between family members for dividing family property on death or divorce.
- Contracts for the sale of land.
- Contracts for the sale of shares.

Where there has been a change in circumstances

This covers the situation where the statement was true when made, but became false by the time that the contract was formed:

KEY CASE

With v. *O'Flanagan* [1936] Ch 575

Concerning: misrepresentation; change of circumstances

Facts

During the course of negotiations for the sale of a medical practice, the vendor made representations to the purchaser that it was worth £2,000 a year. By the time the contract was signed, four months later, the value of the practice had declined to only £250 because the vendor had been ill.

Legal principle

Lord Wright MR stated that:

'... if a statement has been made which is true at the time, but which during the course of negotiations becomes untrue, then the person who knows that it has become untrue is under an obligation to disclose to the other the change of circumstances.'

▶

> **KEY CASE**
>
> Therefore, the failure of the vendor to disclose the state of affairs to the purchaser amounted to a misrepresentation.

Half-truths

Where a statement does not represent the whole truth (in other words, if there are other facts which affect the weight of those truths stated) then this may be regarded as a misrepresentation. For instance, in *Notts Patent Brick and Tile Co.* v. *Butler* (1886) a purchaser of property asked the vendor's solicitor whether the land was subject to any restrictive covenants. The solicitor replied that he was not aware of any. However, while this was true, the solicitor's lack of awareness was a result of his failure to read the relevant documents (rather than having made due enquiry). This amounted to a misrepresentation.

Where there is a fiduciary relationship

A fiduciary relationship between the parties to a contract imposes a duty of disclosure. Examples of such relationships include:

- agent – principal
- solicitor – client
- partners in a partnership
- doctor – patient.

Misrepresentation by conduct

A misrepresentation can be made by conduct rather then being written or oral:

> **KEY CASE**
>
> ### *Spice Girls* v. *Aprilia World Service BV* (2000) The Times, 5 April
>
> **Concerning: misrepresentation; change of circumstances**
>
> #### Facts
>
> Aprilia (moped manufacturers) contracted with the Spice Girls to sponsor a concert tour. The group had appeared in promotional material before Aprilia entered into the contract on 6 May 1998. This contract was based on the representation (made at the promotional photo-call) that all five members of the band, each with their distinctive image, would continue working together. Geri Halliwell ('Ginger Spice') left the band on 29 May 1998.

▶

KEY CASE	**Legal principle**
	There had been misrepresentation by conduct, since the participation of all five band members in the commercial had induced Aprilia into entering the contract.

EXAM TIP

If you are considering misrepresentation by conduct in a problem question, think about what impression is given by the facts: e.g. by appearing together to promote a concert tour, the Spice Girls gave the impression that they had an ongoing working relationship when, in reality, they knew that a split was forthcoming. If the impression given is false, this may amount to misrepresentation by conduct.

Made prior to the contract

The misrepresentation must be made *before* the contract is formed. A statement that is made after formation of the contract cannot be actionable (*Roscorla* v. *Thomas* (1842)).

Inducement into the contract

Finally, the statement must be an inducement to the other party to enter into the contract. In other words, the claimant must have relied on, or been induced to enter the contract by, the false statement of fact. Therefore:

■ the claimant must have known of the existence of the statement, and
■ the statement must have materially affected the claimant's judgement such that the claimant was induced by it or acted in reliance upon it.

Existence of the statement

The misrepresentation must be made to the party that was misled (*Peek* v. *Gurney* (1873)) unless the claimant can establish that the party that made the statement knew that it would be passed on to them. In this case, the party making the statement can be liable in misrepresentation (*Pilmore* v. *Hood* (1838); *Clef Aquitaine* v. *Laporte Materials (Barrow) Ltd* (2000)). It follows in either case that the claimant must be aware of the representation:

Horsefall v. *Thomas* (1862) 1 H & C 90

Concerning: misrepresentation; claimant must be aware of the representation

Facts

The buyer of a gun did not examine it prior to purchase. A defect in the gun was concealed.

Legal principle

The court held that concealing the defect in the gun did not affect the claimant's decision to purchase as, since he was unaware of the misrepresentation, he could not have been induced into the contract by it. His claim failed.

Reliance or inducement

The claimant must actually have relied upon or acted upon the representation:

Attwood v. *Small* (1838) 6 Cl & F 232

Concerning: misrepresentation; reliance

Facts

The purchasers of a mine were told exaggerated statements as to its earning capacity by the vendors. The purchasers had these statements checked by their own expert agents, who erroneously reported them as being correct. Six months after the sale was complete the claimants discovered that the defendants' statement had been false. They sought to rescind the contract with the vendors on the basis of their misrepresentation.

Legal principle

There was no misrepresentation since the purchasers did not rely on the representation made by the vendor. The purchaser had relied on the verification of their agents.

It follows, therefore, that if the claimant knows that the representation is false, then there is no claim in misrepresentation, as there can be no reliance upon a known false statement.

There will be reliance even if the party to whom the representation is made is given an opportunity to verify its truth but chooses not to do so. The misrepresentation will still be considered to be an inducement (*Redgrave* v. *Hurd* (1881)).

Moreover, there will be reliance where the misrepresentation was not the only inducement for the claimant to enter into the contract (*Edgington* v. *Fitzmaurice* (1885)).

Reliance may also be demonstrated by acting upon the representation:

KEY CASE

JEB Fasteners Ltd v. *Marks Bloom & Co.* [1981] 3 All ER 289

Concerning: misrepresentation; acting upon the representation

Facts

The defendants prepared an audited set of accounts for a manufacturing company in which the value of the company's stocks was incorrectly stated. The defendants were aware when they prepared the accounts that the company had liquidity problems and was seeking outside financial support from, amongst others, the claimants. The claimants had reservations about the stock valuation. However, they took over the company for a nominal amount because they would thereby obtain the services of the company's two directors who had considerable experience. The takeover was not as successful as the claimants had wished and they sued the defendants for negligent misrepresentation in the audited accounts.

Legal principle

There was no misrepresentation, since the purchasers wanted to acquire the services of two of the company's directors and would have gone ahead with the purchase even if they had known the true financial state of the company.

Finally, the misrepresentation must be material. This was generally thought to mean that the misrepresentation must have been likely to affect the judgement of a reasonable man in deciding whether to enter the contract. However, in *Museprime Properties Ltd* v. *Adhill Properties Ltd* (1990), the judge considered that, even where the claimant's reliance upon a representation has been unreasonable, if the representation had nonetheless induced the claimant to enter into the contract then the representation was held to be material.

Types of misrepresentation

Not all misrepresentations are as grave as each other. There is a sliding scale of seriousness (See Figure 6.1).

Figure 6.1

Fraudulent misrepresentation

Fraudulent misrepresentation was considered in *Derry* v. *Peek*.

KEY CASE

Derry v. *Peek* (1889) LR 14 App Cas 337

Concerning: fraudulent misrepresentation

Facts

The defendants were directors of the Plymouth, Devonport and District Tramways Co. Ltd, which was authorised by statute to run tramways by animal power, or, with the consent of the Board of Trade, by steam power. The prospectus issued by the company indicated that steam power would be used, but the Board of Trade refused its consent. The claimant, acting in reliance upon the representation in the prospectus, had obtained shares in the company.

Legal principle

This case concerned the tort of deceit. The House of Lords held that, in the absence of any evidence that the defendants believed the statement in the prospectus to be untrue, they had not committed the tort of deceit.

Lord Herschell considered the meaning of 'fraudulent' as follows:

'... fraud is proved when it is shown that a false representation has been made (1) knowingly, or (2) without belief in its truth, or (3) recklessly, careless whether it be true or false. Although I have treated the second and third as distinct cases, I think the third is but an instance of the second, for one who makes a statement under such circumstances can have no real belief in the truth of what he states. To prevent a false statement being fraudulent, there must, I think, always be an honest belief in its truth.'

Therefore, honest belief, or lack thereof, is at the heart of fraud. Motive is irrelevant (*Akerhielm* v. *De Mare* (1959)). Recklessness does not, of itself, establish fraud, unless it is a blatant disregard for the truth (and is therefore sufficiently serious to be dishonest) (*Thomas Witter Ltd* v. *TBP Industries Ltd* (1996)).

Negligent misrepresentation

Historically, all misrepresentations which were not fraudulent were considered innocent and, as such, gave rise to no cause of action or remedy at common law. However, there are now actions available for certain non-fraudulent misrepresentations at both common law and statute.

Common law

At common law, damages may be recoverable for negligent misstatement which causes financial loss:

KEY CASE

Hedley Byrne & Co. Ltd v. Heller & Partners Ltd [1963] 2 All ER 575

Concerning: negligent misrepresentation

Facts

The claimant was an advertising agency which had asked the defendant bank for a reference in respect of one of its clients, which was a customer of the bank. The bank replied that the agency could assume that its client would be able to meet its financial obligations. The agency's client was in fact unable to do so.

Legal principle

The House of Lords held that negligent statements could attract liability and that this liability would extend to pure economic (financial) loss. This liability arises if:

■ the defendant carelessly makes a false statement to the claimant; and
■ the circumstances are such that it is reasonable to assume that the statement will be relied upon; and
■ there is a 'special relationship' between the parties.

This 'special relationship' (which does not have to be contractual) between the parties gives rise to a duty of care and generally exists where the party making the statement:

■ has special knowledge or skill in relation to the subject matter of the contract (*Harris* v. *Wyre Forest District Council* (1988)); and

■ can reasonably foresee that the other party will rely upon their statement (*Chaudry v. Prabhakar* (1988)).

The party must, in fact, rely upon the statement and the party which has made the statement must be aware of this (*Smith* v. *Eric S. Bush* (1990)).

The principles of negligent misstatement stated *obiter* in *Hedley Byrne* v. *Heller* have been applied so that it is now the case that liability arises for negligent misstatement which has induced a party to enter into a contract. This may also cover representations as to a future state of affairs.

KEY CASE

Esso Petroleum & Co. Ltd v. *Marden &* [1976] QB 801

Concerning: negligent misrepresentation

Facts

During the negotiations for the franchise of a petrol station, a representative of Esso stated that the station would sell 200,000 gallons of fuel annually based on its proximity to a busy road. Marden contracted on the basis of this statement. The local authority then insisted that the pumps and entrance to the petrol station were moved such that the station would be accessible only from side streets and unseen by passing trade. As a result, actual sales were around 85,000 gallons. Marden lost all his money in the enterprise. Esso claimed for back rent. Marden argued that, *inter alia*, the relationship with Esso was special and created a duty of care under the *Hedley Byrne* principle.

Legal principle

The court held that the failure to disclose the change in circumstances amounted to negligent misrepresentation under the *Hedley Byrne* principle. Per Lord Denning:

'... If a man, who has or professes to have special knowledge or skill, makes a representation by virtue thereof to another ... with the intention of inducing him to enter a contract with him, he is under a duty to use reasonable care to see that the representation is correct ... If he negligently gives unsound advice or misleading information or expresses an erroneous opinion, and thereby induces the other side into a contract with him, he is liable [in negligent misstatement].'

EXAM TIP

When answering a problem question, look out for any hint in the facts that one party possesses special skill or knowledge, e.g. they may be described as being a member of a particular profession such as an accountant, or is acting in such a way

▶

that they give the impression that they have special skill and knowledge, as this is a trigger for you to consider whether negligent misrepresentation is established.

Statute

The Misrepresentation Act 1967 provides a statutory basis for a claim in respect of non-fraudulent misrepresentation:

Misrepresentation Act 1967, section 2(1)

'Where a person has entered into a contract after a misrepresentation has been made to him by another party thereto and as a result thereof he has suffered loss, then, if the person making the misrepresentation would be liable to damages in respect thereof had the misrepresentation been made fraudulently, that person shall be so liable notwithstanding that the misrepresentation was not made fraudulently, unless he proves that he had reasonable ground to believe and did believe up to the time the contract was made that the facts represented were true.'

The key differences between the common law and statutory claims are illustrated in the following table:

Common law	Statute
Burden of proof on claimant	Burden of proof on defendant
No contract required	Contract required
Special relationship required	No special relationship required

Therefore, where there is a contract and an action under the *Hedley Byrne* principle might not be straightforward, then the statutory claim under section 2(1) of the Misrepresentation Act 1967 would be preferable since it is for the defendant to prove that he had a continuing honest belief in his statement. This may be difficult to do (see, e.g., *Howard Marine Dredging Co. Ltd* v. *A. Ogden & Sons (Excavating) Ltd* (1978) QB 574 in which the Court of Appeal – Lord Denning dissenting – held that there was insufficient evidence to sustain an argument that there was honest belief in a representation).

EXAM TIP

Make sure you have a good understanding of the circumstances in which common law and statutory misrepresentation apply as it is important to select the correct area of law for discussion.

Innocent misrepresentation

Following the developments in *Hedley Byrne* and section 2(1) of the Misrepresentation Act 1967, it follows that an innocent misrepresentation is one which is made in the belief that it is true and that there are reasonable grounds for that belief.

Remedies for misrepresentation

The remedies that are available for misrepresentation depend on the type of misrepresentation that has occurred (see Figure 6.2).

Figure 6.2

Rescission

Rescission is an equitable remedy. It involves setting the contract aside and is available regardless of the type of misrepresentation that has occurred. Rescinded contracts are terminated *ab initio*: in other words, from the very start. It follows that the object of rescission is to put the contracting parties into the position that they would have been in if the contract had never existed at all. However, there are limitations on its availability (so-called 'bars to rescission'):

▊ affirmation
▊ lapse of time
▊ rights of third parties
▊ impossible to restore parties to original positions
▊ damages in lieu of rescission is a better remedy.

Affirmation

Rescission will not be available if the claimant has affirmed the contract either by expressly stating that they intend to continue with it or by acting in such a way that the intention to continue with the contract can be implied from their conduct. Affirmation must be done with full knowledge of the representation and the right to rescind the contract (*Long* v. *Lloyd* (1958)).

Lapse of time

Where there has been too great a lapse of time before rescission is sought, this may be evidence of affirmation and thus a bar to rescission. For fraudulent misrepresentation, the time runs from the point at which the fraud was discovered (or could have been discovered with reasonable diligence). For non-fraudulent misrepresentation, the time runs from the date of the contract itself, not the date of discovery (*Leaf* v. *International Galleries* (1950)).

Rights of third parties

Rescission is not available where a third party has gained bona fide rights for value in property under the contract (*Oakes* v. *Turquand* (1867)). Therefore, if goods are obtained by misrepresentation and sold in good faith to a third party, the contract cannot then be rescinded to allow the party to whom the misrepresentation was made to recover the goods from the third party (*White* v. *Garden* (1851)).

Restitution is impossible

Since the aim of rescission is to restore the parties to their pre-contractual position, it follows that it cannot be available as a remedy where it is impossible to do so. This may occur if the nature of the subject matter of the contract has changed (*Clarke* v. *Dickson* (1858); *Vigers* v. *Pike* (1842)). However, there is some discretion available to the court. Precise restoration is not required as long as substantial restoration is possible (*Head* v. *Tattersall* (1871)). Diminution in value of the property is not, of itself, a bar to rescission (*Armstrong* v. *Jackson* (1917)).

Damages in lieu of rescission is a better remedy

Rescission may not be available if the court considers that damages in lieu of rescission provides a better remedy. This arises by virtue of section 2(2) of the Misrepresentation Act 1967:

KEY STATUTE

Misrepresentation Act 1967, section 2(2)

'Where a person has entered into a contract after a misrepresentation has been made to him otherwise than fraudulently, and he would be entitled, by reason of the misrepresentation, to rescind the contract, then, if it is claimed, in any proceedings arising out of the contract, that the contract ought to be or has been rescinded, the court or arbitrator may declare the contract subsisting and award damages in lieu of rescission, if of opinion that it would be equitable to do so, having regard to the nature of the misrepresentation and the loss that would be caused by it if the contract were upheld, as well as to the loss that rescission would cause to the other party.'

In *William Sindall plc* v. *Cambridgeshire County Council* (1994) the court considered that the damages awarded under section 2(2) should be 'the difference in value between what [the claimant] was misled into believing he was acquiring and the value of what he in fact received'.

Damages

Damages for misrepresentation are assessed on principles of tort law:

Fraudulent misrepresentation

For fraudulent misrepresentation, the claim arises in the tort of deceit. The intention is to return the claimant to the position that they would have been in if the misrepresentation had not been made – that is the 'out of pocket' financial loss (*McConnel* v. *Wright* (1903)) as well as a possible element for 'opportunity cost' (such as the loss of profits that resulted from reliance on the misrepresentation – *East* v. *Maurer* (1991)).

The claimant can recover damages for all direct loss regardless of foreseeability: in *Doyle* v. *Olby (Ironmongers) Ltd* (1969) Lord Denning stated that 'the defendant is bound to make reparation for all the damage flowing from the fraudulent inducement'. This was affirmed by the House of Lords in *Smith New Court Securities Ltd* v. *Scrimgeour Vickers (Asset Management) Ltd* (1997).

Negligent misrepresentation

In negligent misrepresentation, a claim can be made under the principles from *Hedley Byrne* v. *Heller* (provided that the tort can be established). Here (unlike in the tort of deceit) only reasonably foreseeable losses may be recovered.

Alternatively, the claimant may claim under section 2(1) of the Misrepresentation Act 1967 if there is a contract. Damages under section 2(1) are assessed on the same basis as fraudulent misrepresentation (*Royscot Trust Ltd* v. *Rogerson* (1991)).

Innocent misrepresentation

There is no common law action for innocent misrepresentation although rescission is still possible as an equitable remedy. If rescission is available, then damages in lieu may be available under section 2(2) of the Misrepresentation Act 1967.

FURTHER THINKING

Although it contains only three sections, the Misrepresentation Act 1967 has generated a significant volume of case law as the courts have tried to interpret its requirements. In order to obtain an insight into the difficulties posed by this Act and the way in which they have been tackled by the courts, read O'Sullivan, J.,

'Remedies for Misrepresentation: Up in the Air Again' (2001) 60 *Cambridge Law Journal* 231. This article provides a clear outline of the leading cases and their approach to interpretation and would be useful reading in preparation for an essay question.

Mistake

There is no general 'doctrine' of mistake. However, there are certain situations where a contract may be void at common law as a result of a mistake made by the contracting parties. There are three categories of mistake:

■ **Common mistake**: where both parties make the same mistake.
■ **Mutual mistake**: where the parties are at cross-purposes, but each believes that the other is in agreement.
■ **Unilateral mistake**: where one party is mistaken and the other knows and takes advantage of the mistake.

Where a mistake is not operative, then equity may also intervene.
The effect of mistake on a contract can be depicted as shown in Figure 6.3.

Figure 6.3

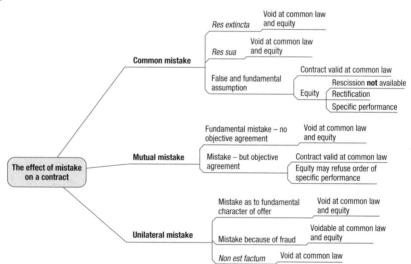

Common mistake

With common mistake there is complete agreement between the parties, but both are mistaken in regard to a fundamental point as to the existence or quality of the subject matter of the contract or the possibility of performing the contract. There are three different types of common mistake:

- *res extincta*
- *res sua*
- mistake as to quality.

Res extincta

Res extincta refers to a mistake as to the *existence* of the subject matter of the contract.

KEY CASE

Couturier v. _Hastie_ (1856) 5 HL Cas 673

Concerning: common mistake; _res extincta_

Facts

This contract was for the sale of a cargo of Indian corn in transit. Both parties believed that the corn existed at the time of the contract. In fact, during the voyage, the cargo became overheated and fermented such that it was unfit to be carried further. The captain of the ship sold the cargo. This was customary practice. The claimant claimed on the basis that the defendant accepted the risk and should pay for the corn.

Legal principle

The court declared the contract void. Although there was no specific mention of mistake the court considered that common sense dictated that if the subject matter of the contract did not exist at formation, then the contract did not exist either.

This proposition is now contained in section 6 of the Sale of Goods Act 1979.

KEY STATUTE

Sale of Goods Act 1979, section 6

'Where there is a contract for the sale of specific goods, and the goods without the knowledge of the seller have perished at the time when the contract is made, the contract is void.'

This principle may also apply where the parties contract on the basis of a mistaken assumption: in *Scott* v. *Coulson* (1903) the claimant contracted to sell to the defendant a policy of life insurance on the life of a third party. However, at the time of the contract, the third party was already dead. The contract was set aside.

However, where one party actually *warrants* the existence of the subject matter (and therefore carries the risk of its non-existence) then the contract is valid. The mistake does not affect the contract: *McRae* v. *Commonwealth Disposals Commission* (1951).

Res sua

Res sua refers to a shared mistake as to the *ownership* of the subject matter of the contract.

KEY CASE

Cooper v. *Phibbs* (1867) LR 2 HL 149

Concerning: common mistake; *res sua*

Facts

An uncle mistakenly told his nephew that he (the uncle) was entitled to a fishery. After the uncle had died, the nephew, acting in reliance on his late uncle's statement, entered into an agreement to rent the fishery from the uncle's daughters. However, the fishery actually belonged to the nephew himself.

Legal principle

The House of Lords held that the contract was void at common law.

Mistake as to quality

A common mistake as to the *quality* of the subject matter of the contract is not sufficiently fundamental to be an operative mistake at common law. In *Leaf* v. *International Galleries* (1950), a gallery sold a painting. Both the gallery and the purchaser believed that it was a Constable. Five years later, while trying to resell the painting, the purchaser found out that it was not a Constable and therefore worth considerably less. The court held that, in the absence of actionable misrepresentation or assumption of risk, the contract was valid.

KEY CASE

Bell v. *Lever Brothers* [1932] AC 161

Concerning: common mistake; mistake as to quality

Facts

Lever Brothers entered into an agreement with one of its employees (Bell) to leave the company in exchange for £30,000 compensation. It was later revealed that there were in fact grounds for termination without compensation at the time of the agreement as Bell had previously breached his contract of employment (but had forgotten about the breaches).

Legal principle

The House of Lords held that the contract was valid since the mistake was not 'of such a fundamental character as to constitute an underlying assumption without which the parties would not have made the contract they in fact made'.

However, there are some indications that the courts may find that a contract is void for common mistake as to quality if the mistake is sufficiently fundamental: *Great Peace (Shipping) Ltd* v. *Tsavliris (Salvage) International Ltd* (2002).

EXAM TIP

The important consideration here is whether the mistake is so fundamental that a party to the contract would not have entered into an agreement if they were in possession of accurate information. Think about the facts in a problem question and put yourself in the position of the mistaken party: would you have gone ahead with the contract if you knew the reality of the situation? Although this can be a good technique to use to assess whether a mistake is fundamental, do not forget to be guided by principles derived from case law.

Mutual mistake

With mutual mistake, the contracting parties are at cross-purposes, but each believes that the other party is in agreement. They do not realise that there is a misunderstanding as to:

■ the terms of the contract; or
■ the subject matter of the contract.

Terms of the contract

The courts will try to make objective sense of the contract wherever possible.

Raffles v. *Wichelhaus* (1864) 2 Hurl & C 906

Concerning: mutual mistake; terms of the contract

Facts

The claimant entered into a contract to sell some bales of cotton to the defendant. The contract specified that the cotton would be arriving on the ship

Peerless from Bombay. There were two ships named *Peerless* arriving from Bombay, one departing in October and another departing in December. The defendant, according to statements presented in court, thought the contract was for cotton on the October ship while the claimant thought the contract was for the cotton on the December ship. When the December *Peerless* arrived, the claimant tried to deliver it. The defendant repudiated the agreement, saying that their contract was for the cotton on the October *Peerless*.

The claimant sued for breach of contract.

Legal principle

The court considered whether a reasonable third party would interpret the contract in line with the understanding of one or the other of the parties. If the court can find a common intention then the contract will be upheld. Here, the court could not determine which *Peerless* was intended in the contract. Therefore the mutual mistake was operative, there was no agreement and the contract was void.

Subject matter of the contract

Where there is mutual misunderstanding as to the subject matter of the contract, then the contract may also be void:

***Scriven Brothers & Co. v. Hindley & Co.* [1913] 3 KB 564**

Concerning: mutual mistake; subject matter of the contract

Facts

The defendants bid at an auction for two lots, believing both to be hemp. In fact Lot A was hemp but Lot B was tow. Tow is of considerably less valuable than hemp. Both lots contained the same mark, 'SL'. The purchasers had been shown bales of hemp as 'samples of the "SL" goods'. Moreover, it was unusual for different goods to be shipped under the same mark.

The defendants declined to pay for Lot B and the sellers sued.

Legal principle

The court considered that a reasonable third party could not determine whether the contract was for hemp or tow. The contract was held to be void.

However, the contract is not void where only one party is mistaken as to the quality of the goods (and performance of the contract is possible): *Smith* v. *Hughes* (1871).

Unilateral mistake

With unilateral mistake, one party is mistaken as to the contract and the other party is aware of the mistake (or the circumstances are such that they may be taken to be aware of the mistake). This is normally a result of a mistake as to one of the following:

▌ identity of one of the contracting parties
▌ terms of the contract
▌ nature of a signed document (*non est factum*).

Identity of one of the contracting parties

If there is a unilateral mistake as to the identity of the person contracted with, the contract will only be void for mistake where:

▌ the identity of the contracting person is of *fundamental importance* to the contract (*Cundy* v. *Lindsay* (1878)); and
▌ this is made clear by the party who is mistaken *before or at the time of* the contract (*Boulton* v. *Jones* (1857)).

Where a contract is made face to face, the contract is considered to be formed with the actual person irrespective of the identity assumed by that party (*Lewis* v. *Averay* (1971)). This is also true where a contract is made through an intermediary *(Shogun Finance Ltd* v. *Hudson* (2004)). Reasonable steps should be taken to check the identity of the other person (*Citibank NA* v. *Brown Shipley & Co. Ltd*; *Midland Bank plc* v. *Brown Shipley & Co. Ltd* (1991)).

Terms of the contract

Where there is a mistaken statement of intent by one party and the other party knows of it, then the mistake is operative and the contract is void.

KEY CASE

Hartog v. *Colin & Shields* [1913] 3 KB 564

Concerning: unilateral mistake; statement of intent

Facts

The defendants were London hide merchants. They had discussed selling the claimant '30,000 hare skins at 10d per skin'. When the final offer was put in writing they mistakenly wrote '30,000 skins @ 10d per lb'. This amounted to around one-third of the price previously discussed. The claimant brought an action to hold the defendants to the written offer.

▶

Legal principle

The court held that the claimant must have realised the defendants' error. Since this error concerned a term of the contract, the contract was void.

A unilateral mistake is operative if:

- one party is mistaken on a material term of the contract without fault (*Sybron Corporation* v. *Rochem* (1984));
- the other party knew, or should reasonably have known, of the mistake (*Wood* v. *Scarth* (1858)).

Nature of a signed document – *non est factum*

Non est factum refers to a unilateral mistake concerning documents as to the *nature* of the document signed.

There must be a fundamental difference between the legal effect of the document signed and that to which the contracting party thought they had signed. The mistake regarding the legal effect of the document must not result from the carelessness of the claimant (*Saunders* v. *Anglia Building Society* (1970)).

Mistake and equity

If a mistake is not operative, then equity may be used in three possible ways:

- rescission
- rectification
- refusal to make order of specific performance.

Rescission

Rescission is available where it is unconscionable to allow one party to take advantage of the mistake (*Solle* v. *Butcher* (1950)). However, it is not available for common mistake (*Great Peace (Shipping) Ltd* v. *Tsavliris (Salvage) International Ltd* (2002)).

Rectification

The court may rectify documents to conform to the real agreement between the parties if there is evidence that the contract does not reflect the prior agreement reached by the parties (*Joscelyne* v. *Nissen* (1970)).

Refusal to make order of specific performance

Since equitable remedies (such as specific performance) are at the discretion of the court, the court may refuse to grant such remedies. Therefore, specific performance may be refused in the case of a mistake made by one party if:

■ it would be inequitable to compel that party to perform their contractual obligations; or
■ the other party knew and took advantage of that mistake (*Webster* v. *Cecil* (1861)); or
■ the mistake resulted from misrepresentation by the other party.

However, the court will not withhold an order of specific performance to save the mistaken party from a bad bargain (*Tamplin* v. *James* (1916)).

■ Illegality

Illegality is a vitiating factor which concerns itself with the character of the contract, unlike misrepresentation or mistake which are more concerned with whether it was entered into voluntarily.

REVISION NOTE

The extent to which illegality is covered as a vitiating factor varies between courses. Therefore, some courses will consider illegality in greater depth than is possible within this revision guide. You should therefore check your course syllabus carefully to see if you need to do some further revision in this area.

Considerations of public policy are a major factor. Contracts may be void or illegal at common law or by statute:

	Common law	Statute
Illegal	In general those which are harmful on grounds of public policy as impinging upon freedom of contract, such as:	Contracts declared illegal upon formation by statute for public policy reasons (*Re Mahmood and Ispahani* (1921))
	Contracts to commit crime or benefit from crime (*Allen* v. *Rescous* (1676))	Void *ab initio* – therefore unenforceable.
	Contracts to defraud Inland Revenue (now HM Revenue & Customs) (*Napier* v. *National Business Agency* (1951))	Contracts formed legally but performed illegally (*Hughes* v. *Asset Managers plc* (1995))
	Contracts concerning corruption in public life (*Parkinson* v. *College of Ambulance Ltd* (1925))	Where one party is unaware of illegality, some remedies may be available, particularly where the illegality is a peripheral issue.
	Contracts to promote immorality (*Pearce* v. *Brooks* (1866))	
Void	Contracts ousting the jurisdiction of the courts	Restrictive trading agreements ('solus' agreements)
	Contracts undermining marriage	(Restrictive Trade Practices Act 1976; Competition Act 1998; Articles 81 EC and 82 EC)
	Contracts in restraint of trade (*Esso Petroleum Co. Ltd* v. *Harper's Garage (Stourport) Ltd* (1968))	Consequences depend on wording of statute; if silent, common law rules apply
	Offending clause may be removed if possible without altering the meaning of the contract, provided the outcome is not abhorrent to public policy	

Chapter Summary:
Putting it all together

☐ Can you tick all the points from the revision checklist at the beginning of this chapter?

☐ Take the **end-of-chapter quiz** on the Companion Website.

☐ Test your knowledge of the cases below with the **revision flashcards** on the website.

☐ Attempt the problem question from the beginning of the chapter using the guidelines below.

☐ Go to the Companion Website to try out other questions.

Answer guidelines

See the problem question at the start of the chapter.

Points to remember when answering this question:

■ This question concerns misrepresentation.

■ You could start by briefly explaining the difference between pre-contractual and contractual statements.

■ Contractual statements are terms of the contract.

■ Representations are pre-contractual statements: if false these are misrepresentations.

■ Actionable misrepresentation must be proved.

■ Define 'actionable' misrepresentation: false statement of material fact by one contracting party to the other before the contract was made which induced the claimant to enter into the contract.

■ You should then consider the factual situation and decide whether any of the statements made were 'actionable' or merely statements of opinion, considering (for instance) *Dimmock* v. *Hallet*, *Bisset* v. *Wilkinson*, *Smith* v. *Land and House Property Corp.*

■ Does Thomas have a duty to verify Rebecca's statement? No (*Redgrave* v. *Hurd*, *Atwood* v. *Small*).

■ Does it matter that the misrepresentation was not the only inducement? Consider *Edgington* v. *Fitzmaurice*.

■ You should distinguish between fraudulent (*Derry* v. *Peek*), negligent (*Hedley Byrne* v. *Heller*, *Esso Petroleum* v. *Marden*) and innocent misrepresentation.

▌ Consider the remedies available at common law and statute:
  – common law: burden of proof on Thomas:
    – fraudulent: damages and/or rescission, consequential damages recoverable if not too remote (*Doyle* v. *Olby, Smith New Court Securities Ltd* v. *Scrimgeour Vickers*); possible to recover for loss of profit (*East* v. *Maurer*);
    – negligent: damages and/or rescission (*Hedley Byrne* v. *Heller*), special relationship needed (*Esso Petroleum*);
    – innocent: no remedy at common law, only in equity;
  – Misrepresentation Act 1967, section 2(1):
    – negligent: burden of proof shifts onto defendant (*Howard Marine* v. *Ogden*);
    – damages and/or rescission; measure of damages same as for fraudulent misrepresentation (*Royscot Trust Ltd* v. *Rogerson*);
  – Misrepresentation Act 1967, section 2(2):
    – negligent or wholly innocent: damages (in the form of indemnity) in lieu of rescission if rescission is barred (state the bars) or is too harsh a remedy (*William Sindall* v. *Cambridgeshire County Council*).
▌ Preferred action falls under Misrepresentation Act, section 2(1); damages assessed on tort basis to put Thomas into the position he was in before the contract was made.

Make your answer really stand out:
▌ There are many propositions of law to consider in answering this problem. It is important to break your answer down into as many small pieces as possible. For each proposition of law you should provide suitable case authority.
▌ Ensure that you consider all the pertinent facts given to you in the question. Examiners seldom introduce facts as 'red herrings'. Your ability to apply the law to the facts effectively shows good depth of understanding and analysis.
▌ You might also consider the possibility of Rebecca's statement being a term of the contract, in which case Thomas could claim for all foreseeable losses to put him into the position he would have been in had the contract been properly performed.

7
Duress and undue influence

Duress
- Actual or threatened violence to the person
- Threats to property
- Economic duress

Duress and undue influence

Undue influence
- Actual undue influence
- Presumed undue influence – special relationship
- Presumed undue influence – no special relationship
- Undue influence and third parties
- Remedies

A printable version of this topic map is available from www.pearsoned.co.uk/lawexpress

Revision Checklist

What you need to know:

- [ ] The nature of duress and the effect that it has on a contract
- [ ] The development of duress from threats of personal violence to threats towards property
- [ ] The evolution of economic duress and the factors that determine its availability
- [ ] The circumstances that amount to undue influence and how this differs from duress
- [ ] The different classes of undue influence and their operation.

Introduction:
Duress and undue influence

It is of fundamental importance that parties to a contract enter into the agreement voluntarily rather than as a result of pressure (duress) or manipulation (undue influence).

This chapter will explore the operation of the common law doctrine of duress and the equitable doctrine of undue influence. An understanding of these doctrines is important to your understanding of contract law as duress and undue influence render an otherwise valid contract voidable on the action of the wronged party, which means that the party who has been subjected to duress or undue influence can avoid being bound by the contract.

Essay question advice

An essay question may focus on these specific areas, e.g. you may encounter a question looking at the evaluation of the law on economic duress, or may ask in general terms about the ways in which otherwise binding contractual obligations may be avoided. If the latter type of question arises, it would be important to remember that it is not only duress and undue influence that render the contract voidable so consideration should also be given to topics such as mistake and misrepresentation.

Problem question advice

Duress and undue influence are popular problem question topics. They may appear in combination with each other, to test the student's ability to differentiate between the two doctrines, or in combination with some topic that enables a claimant to avoid being bound by the contract, such as misrepresentation or mistake. Look out for evidence of pressure (duress) or persuasion (undue influence) in the facts of the problem as this should trigger a consideration of these topics.

Sample question

Could you answer this question? Below is a typical problem question that could arise on this topic. Guidelines on answering the question are included at the end of the chapter, whilst a sample essay question and guidance on tackling it can be found on the Companion Website.

Problem question

Mrs Smith is a 72-year-old widow. She owns a freehold house, valued at £600,000. Five years ago she took in Mr Jones as a lodger. She soon came to trust Mr Jones and let him manage her financial affairs. However, Mrs Smith found out that Mr Jones had served a prison sentence for theft. Two years ago, Mr Jones persuaded Mrs Smith to transfer a one-third share in her house to him. Mrs Smith did so because she was beginning to be fearful of Mr Jones.

Six months later, Mr Jones decided that he wanted to start a new business selling double-glazing. Since he was unable to raise the necessary start-up capital on his own, he persuaded Mrs Smith to put up her remaining two-thirds share of the house as security against a bank loan in his favour. Mrs Smith signed the necessary documents at the bank in the presence of Mr Jones. Now, seven months later, Mr Jones's business venture has collapsed and he is no longer able to make payments on the loan. The bank now intends to take possession of the house.

Advise Mrs Smith whether she might be able to have any of the agreements set aside.

Duress

It is an essential characteristic of contract law that the parties enter into an agreement voluntarily. As such, a party who has been coerced into entering into a contract may be able to avoid the obligations of the contract by reliance upon duress, although much depends on the sort of pressure that has been applied to the claimant.

Actual or threatened violence to the person

Historically, the only sort of pressure that the courts were prepared to recognise as amounting to duress involved personal violence or threats of personal violence.

KEY CASE

Barton v. *Armstrong* [1975] 2 All ER 465

Concerning: duress and threats of violence

Facts

The claimant was the Managing Director of a company of which the defendant was the former Chairman. The defendant threatened to kill the claimant if he did not purchase shares from the defendant. The claimant purchased the shares but sought a declaration that the transaction was void for duress. There was evidence to suggest that the claimant had been partly influenced by the threats and partly motivated by business considerations as the purchase of the shares was a good move for him and the company.

Legal principle

The court held that the contract was voidable because the threats of personal violence were a factor in the claimant's decision to purchase the shares even though he may have entered into the contract even without threats being made. In cases involving threats of violence, the onus was on the defendant to establish that these threats made no contribution to the claimant's decision to enter into a contract.

It is clear that once actual or threatened violence has been established, the claimant will be able to avoid the contract unless the defendant succeeds in the onerous task of establishing that these threats played no part whatsoever on the claimant's decision to enter into the contract. Therefore, as long as threats of violence are *a* reason that the claimant entered into the contract, duress will be established even though threats of violence were not the *only* reason.

Threats to property

For many years, the courts refused to accept that threats to damage or remove property would amount to duress. It is likely that this was because the pressure involved does not seem sufficient to amount to compulsion to enter into a contractual arrangement. For example, in *Skeate* v. *Beale* (1840), the claimant only paid the amount demanded as the defendant threatened to seize goods if payment was not forthcoming. Irrespective of this, the court refused to accept that this was sufficient to amount to duress.

This approach has been rejected and the courts now recognise that threats directed at property may amount to duress. This principle was stated by Kerr J in *Occidental Worldwide Investment Corporation* v. *Skibs A/S Avanti (The Siboen and The Sibotre)* (1976):

> 'If I should be compelled to sign a . . . contract for a nominal but legally sufficient consideration under an imminent threat of having my house burnt down or a valuable picture slashed through without any threat of physical violence to anyone, I do not think that the law should uphold the agreement . . . The true question is ultimately whether or not the agreement in question is to be regarded as having been concluded voluntarily.'

Economic duress

The expansion of duress to include threats to property that was stated in *The Siboen and The Sibotre* paved the way for the development of the concept of economic duress.

> **KEY CASE**
>
> ### *North Ocean Shipping Co.* v. *Hyundai Construction Co.* (*The Atlantic Baron*) [1979] QB 705
>
> **Concerning: duress by economic pressure**
>
> **Facts**
>
> A contract existed for the construction of a boat (*The Atlantic Baron*) but the shipbuilders sought to increase the price after building had commenced due to fluctuations in the exchange rate. The purchaser did not want to agree to the variation in terms but feared that refusal would delay the completion of the boat which would have jeopardised a lucrative charter agreement that was being negotiated on the basis of the original completion date of the boat. The purchaser paid the increased price but, eight months after delivery of the boat, sought to recover the additional sum by claiming that their agreement had been obtained by duress.

Legal principle

It was held that pressure of this nature could amount to duress. The court held that the essence of duress was that there had been 'compulsion of the will' and this could arise just as much from economic pressure as it could from threats of violence. In this case, the claim was unsuccessful, not due to the nature of the pressure but due to the delay in commencing action.

Economic duress simply refers to the focus of the pressure: rather than threats being made to harm a person, the threat is directed towards their financial well-being. This does not have to be a direct 'I'll bankrupt your business if you don't sign this contract' sort of threat. Most instances of economic duress are indirect: for example, 'I will not do business with you unless you reduce your prices by half'. The essence of duress is the 'do this or else' pressure but it does not have to be expressed as a direct threat provided there is evidence of sufficient compulsion.

The principle of economic duress was accepted in subsequent cases but there has been some elaboration on the requirements that must be satisfied.

Pao On v. *Lau Yiu Long* [1980] AC 614

Concerning: the requirements of economic duress

Facts

The claimants threatened not to proceed with the sale of shares unless the defendants agreed to renegotiation on other peripheral issues. The defendants wanted to avoid litigation and were anxious to reach agreement for the sale of the shares so agreed. The claimants tried to enforce the agreement but the defendants resisted on the basis of duress. The Privy Council found in favour of the claimants on the basis that the facts disclosed ordinary commercial pressure that was not sufficient to amount to duress.

Legal principle

The Privy Council stated that duress requires 'coercion of the will which vitiates consent' so that any seeming agreement was given involuntarily. Lord Scarman identified a list of factors that indicated that duress was established:

- Did the person who claims to have been coerced protest at the time?
- Did he have an alternative course of action open to him?
- Did he have access to independent advice?
- Did he take steps to avoid the contract after it was formed?

Lord Scarman identified these factors in order to ascertain whether the innocent party's agreement was involuntary. The factors themselves seem reasonable in identifying duress: we would expect a party who had been forced into an agreement to object at the time and to try to escape the obligation as soon as possible afterwards. Equally, it does not seem reasonable to categorise a situation as duress if the innocent party had other alternatives available to them as choice implies voluntary decision-making. Whilst the factors themselves cannot be criticised, later cases did take issue with Lord Scarman's assertion that duress involved an involuntary decision.

KEY CASE

Universal Tankships v. *International Transport Workers Federation (The Universal Sentinel)* [1983] AC 366

Concerning: the availability of a practical alternative

Facts

A strike organised by ITWF was delaying the production of a ship that was being built for the claimant. ITWF agreed to end the strike if payments were made into its funds. The claimant made a payment but sought to recover the payment on the basis that it was obtained by duress.

Legal principle

It was held that it was not appropriate to talk about duress in terms of involuntary agreement and absence of choice as the innocent party always had a choice even if this was between two unpleasant alternatives, e.g. either pay into the union funds or lose income because the production of the boat is delayed. Lord Diplock stated that it was more appropriate to formulate a test in terms of whether the innocent party was given any practical alternative other than to comply with the other party's demands.

FURTHER THINKING

Econonic duress has generated a great deal of case law and associated academic debate. It would be a valuable contribution to your revision of this topic to read articles that comment on the availability and operation of economic duress as this would help you to prepare for an essay on the topic. Chandler, P.A. 'Economic Duress: Clarity or Confusion?' (1989) *Lloyd's Maritime and Commercial Law Quarterly* 270 provides an insightful critical assessment of some of the earlier case law whilst Smith, S.A., 'Contracting Under Pressure: a Theory of Duress, (1997) 56 *Cambridge Law Journal* 343 provides an interesting discussion of more recent developments in this area of law.

The courts have had to decide what sort of threats will fall within economic duress. It is generally accepted that threats of unlawful action will amount to illegitimate pressure but there are situations in which threats of lawful action may amount to duress if they leave the innocent party with no reasonable alternative other than to acquiesce to the other party's demands.

Threats of unlawful action: *Atlas Express Ltd* v. *Kafco* [1989] 1 All ER 641	Threats of lawful action: *CTN Cash & Carry* v. *Gallagher* [1994] 4 All ER 714
Kafco was a small company that made basket ware and had secured a contract to supply Woolworths. They engaged the claimant to transport the goods but, due to a miscalculation of the costs involved, the claimant increased the price of delivery after the contract had commenced and threatened to cease delivery in breach of contract if the new price was not accepted by the defendant. As failure to supply goods to their major client in the pre-Christmas period would lead to a loss of customer, the defendant felt compelled to accept the higher price but later refused to pay, claiming duress. It was held that this did amount to economic duress as the threat to breach the contract was illegitimate pressure and, due to the timeframe involved, the defendant would have been unable to find an alternative means of ensuring their goods reached the customer.	The defendant supplied leading brands of cigarettes. A consignment of cigarettes ordered by the claimants went astray and the defendant agreed to re-deliver but the goods were stolen prior to delivery. A replacement consignment of cigarettes was delivered to the claimants but the defendant demanded payment for these and the stolen cigarettes. The claimants were told that their credit facilities would be withdrawn if they did not agree to pay for the stolen cigarettes so they agreed but subsequently claimed that the agreement was obtained by duress. The court held that threats of lawful action (to withdraw credit facilities) could amount to illegitimate pressure but that it did not do so in this situation. It was noted that it would require extreme circumstances before 'lawful act duress' would be recognised in a commercial contract.

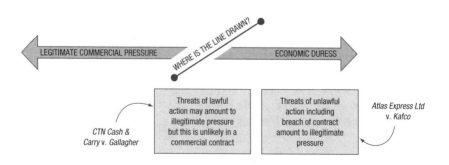

Undue influence

Undue influence is an equitable remedy (and therefore available at the court's discretion). It covers situations where one party has gained an unfair advantage over the other by applying improper pressure (which does not amount to duress at common law). The term 'undue influence' is inherently imprecise and the courts have not provided a precise definition. However, in *Bank of Credit and Commerce International* v. *Aboody* (1990) the courts defined two classes of undue influence:

■ Class 1 – actual undue influence
■ Class 2 – presumed undue influence.

The latter classification was further refined in *Barclays Bank plc* v. *O'Brien* (1993) such that the second class was subdivided as follows:

■ Class 2A – presumed undue influence (arising from a special relationship between the parties)
■ Class 2B – presumed undue influence (no special relationship in the sense of class 2A, but a relationship of trust and confidence).

Actual undue influence

For this class, there are no circumstances in which undue influence may be presumed, so the party alleging undue influence must prove the undue influence: at the time of the contract, they were not able to exercise free will in entering into it:

KEY CASE

Williams v. *Bayley* (1866) LR 1 HL 200

Concerning: actual undue influence

Facts
A young man forged his father's signature on some promissory notes and presented them to a bank, who discovered the forgery. At a meeting between the bank, the father and the son, the bank threatened to prosecute the son unless some satisfactory arrangement could be reached. As a result, the father entered into an agreement to mortgage his property to pay for the notes.

Legal principle
The agreement was set aside on the grounds of undue influence since the father could not be said to have entered the agreement voluntarily.

Aboody also required the party alleging undue influence to show that they had suffered a manifest disadvantage as a result although this requirement was subsequently rejected by the House of Lords in *CIBC Mortgages* v. *Pitt* (1993).

Presumed undue influence – special relationship

Within class 2A, there is a presumption of undue influence which arises when there is a special relationship between the parties. The party alleging undue influence has to prove the existence of the relationship. The burden then falls on the other party to prove that there has been no undue influence. They must show that:

■ the party alleging undue influence had full knowledge of the character and effect of the contract when entering into it; satisfied if
■ the party alleging undue influence had independent and impartial advice before entering into the contract.

Special relationships

There are certain special relationships which give rise to a presumption of class 2A undue influence:

Relationship	Example
Parent – child	*Lancashire Loans Co* v. *Black* (1933)
Religious leader – disciple	*Allcard* v. *Skinner* (1887)
Trustee – beneficiary	*Benningfield* v. *Baker* (1886)
Doctor – patient	*Dent* v. *Bennett* (1839)
Solicitor – client	*Wright* v. *Carter* (1903)

You should note that the relationship between husband and wife was specifically excluded from the class 2A special relationship in *Midland Bank* v. *Shepherd* (1988).

FURTHER THINKING

You might find the exclusion of the husband and wife relationship from the class 2A special relationships surprising. This position is explored in detail by Rosemary Auchmuty in her article 'Men Behaving Badly: an Analysis of English

Undue Influence Cases' (2002) 11 *Social and Legal Studies* 257 which provides a clear explanation of some of the leading cases and argues that the test for undue influence focuses on business relationships, thus failing to protect women who are in a vulnerable position. This may give you some useful ideas for criticisms that can be made about this topic, which could be used in an essay question.

Presumed undue influence – no special relationship

Where there is no special relationship between the parties in the class 2A sense, it is still possible for a party alleging undue influence to give rise to a presumption of undue influence if there is a relationship of trust and confidence.

It most commonly covers the relationship between husband and wife, particularly where one is induced to put up the family home as security for a loan made to the other.

It may also extend to the relationship between a bank and its client (*Lloyds Bank plc* v. *Bundy* (1979)).

Finally, it may apply where the transaction itself 'calls for an explanation' (*Royal Bank of Scotland plc* v. *Etridge (No. 2)* (2001)). In other words, the transaction must constitute a disadvantage sufficiently serious so that evidence is required to rebut the presumption that it was procured by undue influence.

Undue influence and third parties

Many cases involve putting undue influence on a party to induce them into entering into a contract with a third party: for instance, a husband persuading his wife (or vice versa) to enter into an agreement with the bank to provide security for a loan. Here, due to privity of contract, the influencer will have no contractual relationship with the third party.

REVISION NOTE

You may wish to refresh your memory on the doctrine of privity here. See Chapter 3.

However, the third party may have *constructive notice* of the undue influence. If the transaction is one which is:

■ on its face not to the financial advantage of the party seeking to set it aside, and
■ if there is a substantial risk of its having been obtained by undue influence,

then the third party will have constructive notice of undue influence giving the right to set aside the transaction (*Barclays Bank* v. *O'Brien* (1993)).

However, if the transaction is capable of benefiting the party who seeks to set it aside, the third party will *not* have constructive notice of any undue influence which may in fact have existed (*CIBC Mortgages* v. *Pitt* (1993)).

The third party must then show that it took reasonable steps to ensure that the potentially influenced party entered into the transaction freely and with full knowledge of the facts.

The rules which apply where a wife claims that her consent was obtained by the undue influence of her husband were set out in *Royal Bank of Scotland plc* v. *Etridge (No. 2)* (2001).

KEY CASE

Royal Bank of Scotland plc v. Etridge (No. 2) [2001] 4 ALL ER 449

Concerning: undue influence; third parties

Facts

A bank had taken a charge over a wife's property as security for a loan for her husband's business overdraft. The wife signed the charge in the presence of her husband. She had taken advice from a solicitor appointed by the bank, although she thought the solicitor was instructed by her husband. The bank tried to enforce the charge and the wife claimed undue influence.

Legal principle

The House of Lords considered that where a bank hopes to be protected by the fact that the wife will be advised by a solicitor it should communicate directly with the wife informing her that for her own protection it will require written confirmation from a solicitor that the solicitor has explained to her the nature of the documents and the practical implications of the transaction.

Remedies

If undue influence is successfully pleaded, then it renders the contract **voidable**. However, the remedy may be ineffective if the value of the property has changed.

Cheese v. Thomas [1994] 1 FLR 118

Concerning: undue influence; third parties

Facts

Mr Cheese (aged 84) contributed £43,000 towards the purchase of a property costing £83,000. His nephew provided the remainder by way of mortgage. Legal title to the property was in the nephew's sole name. The property was, however, to be solely occupied by Cheese until his death. The nephew defaulted on the mortgage. The uncle claimed undue influence to secure the return of his £43,000.

Legal principle

The court accepted the plea of undue influence. They ordered the house to be sold with the uncle receiving a 43/83 share in the proceeds. However, property prices had slumped and the house was sold for only £55,000, leaving the uncle with only around £28,500.

Chapter Summary:
Putting it all together

☐ Can you tick all the points from the revision checklist at the beginning of this chapter?

☐ Take the **end-of-chapter quiz** on the Companion Website.

☐ Test your knowledge of the cases below with the **revision flashcards** on the website.

☐ Attempt the problem question from the beginning of the chapter using the guidelines below.

☐ Go to the Companion Website to try out other questions.

Answer guidelines

See the problem question at the start of the chapter.

Points to remember when answering this question:

▮ Mrs Smith could claim that as a result of duress by Mr Jones she has transferred a share in her house to him.

■ In order to establish duress to the person Mrs Smith needs to prove that she made this transfer as the result of an actual or threatened violence by Mr Jones (*Barton* v. *Armstrong*).

■ She had found out that Mr Jones had served a prison sentence which by itself is not sufficient to establish duress unless she can prove that he actually threatened her, which he appears not to have done.

■ Therefore it appears that her argument based on duress will be unsuccessful.

■ Undue influence has been classed into three categories as per *BCCI* v. *Aboody* and reaffirmed in *Barclays Bank* v *O'Brien*. Class 1: actual, burden of proof on claimant; class 2A: presumed, arises from a special relationship; class 2B: presumed, no special relationship.

■ Mrs Smith's and Mr Jones's relationship can be assumed to fall into class 2B, Mr Jones being the stronger party (*Lloyds Bank* v. *Bundy*).

■ Mrs Smith is seeking the equitable remedy of rescission. This, however, may no longer be possible because lapse of time is a bar to rescission.

■ As to providing the remaining share in her house as security for Mr Jones's enterprise, Mrs Smith will argue that the bank had constructive notice of the undue influence exercised by Mr Jones upon her (*Barclays Bank* v. *O'Brien*).

■ Did the bank know of the relationship between Mrs Smith and Mr Jones? If the bank did, they could be held to have constructive notice of what was going on since a creditor is aware that a surety places particular trust and confidence in the debtor (*CIBC Mortgages* v. *Pitt*).

■ The nature and extent of the advice to be given by a bank was explained particularly in *Etridge (No. 2)*.

■ As a result it could be argued that Mr Jones may be able to keep the one-third share of Mrs Smith's house. If Mrs Smith can prove that the bank has not taken the reasonable steps required in advising her, the bank will have had constructive notice and the second transaction would be set aside.

Make your answer really stand out:

■ You should point out the difference between the common law principle of duress and the equitable nature of undue influence with discussion of the potential bars to rescission: in particular lapse of time.

■ Treat duress and undue influence separately in relation to each transaction. This will lead to an answer which is well-structured and clear. Combining multiple issues and principles runs the risk of poor expression.

■ Ensure that you use all the relevant facts provided in the question to support your analysis. They are there for a reason.

8
Discharge of a contract

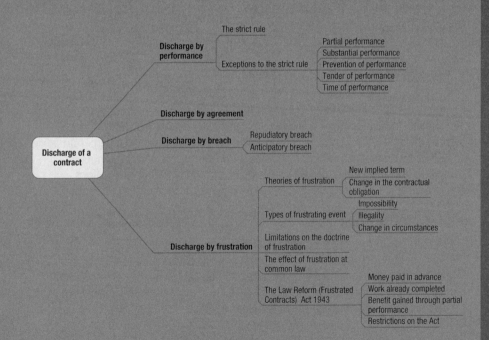

A printable version of this topic map is available from www.pearsoned.co.uk/lawexpress

Revision Checklist

What you need to know:

- [ ] The rule relating to discharge by performance and its exceptions
- [ ] The ways in which a contract may be discharged by agreement between the parties
- [ ] The consequences of breach of contract and the distinction between anticipatory and repudiatory breaches
- [ ] The evolution of the doctrine of frustration and the operation of the Law Reform (Frustrated Contracts) Act 1943.

Introduction:
Discharge

A contract is said to be discharged when it comes to an end.

Contracts normally come to an end when the obligations arising under it are performed. However, under certain circumstances, a contract may be discharged before performance is complete. This chapter will consider discharge by *performance* as well as by *agreement*, where the parties to the contract may end it before it is completed, *breach*, where there is a failure to perform contractual obligations, and *frustration*, where an intervening event prevents performance of the contract.

Essay question advice

Although any of the topics outlined in this chapter could form the basis of an essay question, frustration is a particularly popular topic so it is worth taking time to revise this topic in depth. Be sure that you can outline the elements of the doctrine and make reference to relevant case law to support your explanation. Make sure that you consider the question of whether it is acceptable that an otherwise binding contractual obligation can be avoided simply because unexpected events have made the contract less desirable.

Sample question

Could you answer this question? Below is a typical essay question that could arise on this topic. Guidelines on answering the question are included at the end of the chapter, whilst a sample problem question and guidance on tackling it can be found on the Companion Website.

Essay question

'The object of the doctrine (of frustration) was to give effect to the demands of justice, to achieve a just and reasonable result, to do what is reasonable and fair, as an expedient to escape from injustice where such would result from enforcement of a contract in its literal terms after a significant change in circumstances ...'
   (Bingham LJ in *J Lauritzen AS* v. *Wijsmuller BV (The Super Servant Two)* (1990).
   Critically analyse this statement.

■ Discharge by performance

Strictly speaking, a contract is not discharged until all the obligations arising under it have been performed precisely and exactly.

The strict rule

Although this rule seems to make perfect common sense, it originated in relation to 'entire' contracts which require complete performance of all obligations and can give rise to harsh consequences:

KEY CASE

Cutter v. *Powell* (1795) 6 Term Rep 320

Concerning: discharge by performance

Facts

A seaman agreed to serve on a ship. His wages were to be paid at the end of the voyage. He died mid voyage. His widow attempted to claim his wages.

Legal principle

His widow was not able to recover any of his wages because he had not completed performance of his contractual obligation. (This situation is now provided for by the Merchant Shipping Act 1970.)

This principle has also led to harshness in contracts for the sale of goods:

KEY CASE

Re Moore & Co's and Landauer & Co's Arbitration [1921] 2 KB 519

Concerning: discharge by performance

Facts

The defendants agreed to buy 3,000 tins of canned fruit from the claimants, packed in cases of 30 tins. Part of the consignment was in fact packed in cases of 24 tins. The defendants refused to pay.

Legal principle

The court held that the defendants were entitled to reject the entire consignment as it was not precisely that which was agreed.

This harshness has also now been mitigated by statute, in relation to non-consumer contracts for the sale of goods, by the following two provisions inserted into the Sale of Goods Act 1979 by the Sale and Supply of Goods Act 1994:

KEY STATUTE

Sale of Goods Act 1979, section 15A

'Where in the case of a contract of sale –

(a) the buyer would ... have the right to reject goods by reason of a breach on the part of the seller of a term implied by section 13, 14 or 15 above, but

(b) the breach is so slight that it would be unreasonable for him to reject them,

then, if the buyer does not deal as consumer, the breach is not to be treated as a breach of condition but may be treated as a breach of warranty.'

KEY STATUTE

Sale of Goods Act 1979, section 30(2A)

'A buyer who does not deal as consumer may not –

(a) where the seller delivers a quantity of goods less than he contracted to sell, reject the goods . . ., or

(b) where the seller delivers a quantity of goods larger than he contracted to sell, reject the whole . . .,

if the shortfall or, as the case may be, excess is so slight that it would be unreasonable for him to do so.'

Given the potential for the strict application of the rule to create seemingly unfair results, the courts have developed exceptions to the rule.

Exceptions to the strict rule

Exceptions to the strict rule exist in relation to contracts which impose **severable obligations**.

KEY DEFINITION

A contract imposes **severable obligations** if payment under it is due from time to time as performance of a specified part of the contract is rendered.

(Treitel, G.H. (2003) *The Law of Contract*, London: Sweet & Maxwell, page 784)

Whether or not a contract is severable is a question of interpretation for the court to decide. However, work and materials contracts are usually considered severable.

Partial performance

If a contract is severable, then, provided that the whole contract is not breached, payment can be expected for part performance.

KEY CASE

Roberts v. *Havelock* (1832) 3 B & Ad 404

Concerning: discharge by performance; severable obligations

Facts

A shipwright agreed to repair a ship. The contract did not expressly state when payment was to be made. Before completing the repairs, he requested payment for the work completed to date. The defendants refused to pay.

Legal principle

Since the contract did not require the claimant to complete all the work before payment was made, the court held that the shipwright was not therefore bound to complete the repairs before claiming some payment.

Equally, partial performance may be accepted (*Christy* v. *Row* (1808)). Where partial performance is accepted (and the defendant has free choice whether or not to accept partial performance), then payment is enforceable in respect of the partial performance.

Sumpter v. *Hedges* [1898] 1 QB 673

Concerning: discharge by performance; partial performance

Facts

The claimant agreed to build a house and stables on the defendant's land. He completed around two-thirds of the work and then abandoned the contract. The defendant completed the buildings and refused to pay the claimant for the work done.

Legal principle

The claim failed. The claimant could not recover for the work done since the defendant had no option but to accept the partially completed building.

Substantial performance

Where performance is 'substantial' then the contract may be enforced, although damages may be payable in respect of the incomplete performance. In other words, the amount payable corresponds to the price of the contract minus the cost of the incomplete component:

H. Dakin & Co. Ltd v. *Lee* [1916] 1 KB 566

Concerning: discharge by performance; substantial performance

Facts

The claimants agreed to carry out repairs to the defendant's house. The work was completed but for three minor defects which could be fixed at a small cost. The defendant refused to pay.

KEY CASE

Legal principle

The court upheld the claim since the obligations under the contract had been substantially completed, subject to a deduction of the cost of fixing the outstanding defects.

However, this does give rise to the question of what exactly constitutes 'substantial' performance of contractual obligations. This is a question of fact in each case:

KEY CASE

Bolton v. *Mahadeva* [1972] 2 All ER 1322

Concerning: discharge by performance; substantial performance

Facts

The claimant contracted to install a hot water and central heating system in the defendant's home for £560. There were numerous defects: fumes affected the air in the living room, the house was on average 10 per cent less warm than it should have been, and the deficiency in heat varied from room to room. Overall it would cost £175 to rectify the deficiencies. At first instance, the judge held that the claimant was entitled to the agreed price of £560, but that £175 should be set off against the contract price because of the deficiencies. The defendant appealed.

Legal principle

The Court of Appeal held that there had *not* been substantial performance and therefore the claimant was not entitled to recover anything.

EXAM TIP

When dealing with a problem question, look at the facts and ascertain what was required for complete performance of the contract. This can be used as a benchmark against which to measure what the defendant has actually done; you can then ask, 'how far short of the contractual obligation did the defendant fall?' This will enable you to determine whether there has been substantial performance.

Prevention of performance

Where a party is wrongly prevented from performing its contractual obligations by the other party then the strict rule does not apply. The claimant can either claim damages for breach of contract or on a *quantum meruit* basis for the work done (*Planché* v. *Colburn* (1831)).

Tender of performance

If a party is unable to complete its contractual obligations without the co-operation of the other party then they may make a 'tender of performance' which can be accepted or rejected by the other party. If a tender of performance is rejected, then the party who has tried to complete their contractual obligations will be discharged from further liability.

KEY CASE

***Startup* v. *MacDonald* (1843) 6 Man & C 593**

Concerning: discharge by performance; tender of performance

Facts

The parties contracted for the sale of 10 tons of linseed oil to be delivered 'within the last 14 days of March'. The claimant delivered the oil at 8.30 pm on 31 March and the defendant refused to accept delivery. The defendant subsequently refused to pay.

Legal principle

The claim was successful. The court held that the tender of performance was equivalent to performance and the claimant was entitled to damages for non-acceptance. (Note that now section 29(5) of the Sale of Goods Act 1979 provides that a tender of goods must be made at a 'reasonable' hour – what is reasonable is a question of fact.)

Time of performance

Where a contract fixes a date for performance, it will still only be possible for the contract to be repudiated for breach of the time clause where 'time is of the essence'. This will occur where:

∎ the contract expressly provides that time is of the essence;
∎ time being of the essence can be inferred from the nature of the subject matter and the circumstances of the contract (e.g. a contract for the sale of perishable fresh fruit);
∎ time becomes of the essence: this happens where one party fails to perform in a timely manner and the injured party gives notice that performance must take place within a reasonable time.

If time is of the essence, any delay will amount to repudiation: in *Union Eagle Ltd* v. *Golden Achievement Ltd* (1997) the Privy Council considered that even a 10-minute delay would suffice.

■ Discharge by agreement

Just as a contract can be made by agreement, so it may also be discharged by agreement. However, in general, consideration is required to enforce the agreement to discharge or vary the contract. In some cases, certain formalities will also be required.

REVISION NOTE

You may wish to review your understanding of consideration at this stage. See Chapter 2.

Where consideration is wholly executory (exchanged promises to perform some act in the future) then there is no problem. The parties' exchanged promises to release one another from the contract will be good consideration.

Where consideration is executed (either in part or wholly) then:

■ a deed is required to effect a valid release of the other party; or
■ the other party must provide 'accord and satisfaction' (that is, new consideration)

Alternatively one party could give a voluntary (that is, without consideration) *waiver* to the other not to insist on the precise performance stipulated in the contract. A waiver can be given without formality.

■ Discharge by breach

KEY DEFINITION

A **breach of contract** is committed when a party without lawful excuse fails or refuses to perform what is due from them under the contract, or performs defectively or incapacitates themselves from performing.

(Treitel, G.H. (2003) *The Law of Contract*, London: Sweet & Maxwell, page 832)

REVISION NOTE

It would be useful at this stage to consolidate your revision of the consequences of the breach of conditions, warranties and innominate terms. See Chapter 4.

Repudiatory breach

Repudiatory breaches are serious breaches that entitle the innocent party to consider themselves as being discharged from their obligations under the contract. This is in addition to the standard remedy of damages. In respect of a repudiatory breach, the innocent party may:

■ accept the breach as repudiation of the contract; or
■ affirm the breach (and continue with the contract).

If the breach is treated as repudiatory, this must be communicated to the party in breach of contract (*Vitol SA* v. *Norelf Ltd* (1996)).

Anticipatory breach

Anticipatory breaches occur before performance is due. In essence, an anticipatory breach is where one party makes the other aware of their intention not to perform their contractual obligations. This may be:

■ explicitly (*Hochester* v. *De La Tour* (1853)); or
■ implied by conduct (*Frost* v. *Knight* (1872)).

The innocent party may either accept the repudiation and sue immediately, or wait for the contractual date of performance and sue for breach (if it occurs) in the usual way.

■ Discharge by frustration

KEY DEFINITION

Under the **doctrine of frustration** a contract may be discharged if, after its formation, events occur making its performance impossible or illegal and in certain analogous situations.

(Treitel, G.H. (2003) *The Law of Contract*, London: Sweet & Maxwell, page 866)

Historically, there was an absolute obligation to perform obligations under a contract:

KEY CASE

Paradine v. *Jane* (1647) Aleyn 26

Concerning: frustration; absolute obligations

Facts

Jane owed rent under a lease to Paradine. Jane contended that he had been forced off the land for three years during the term of the lease by an invading army and that he should not therefore be liable to pay rent.

> **KEY CASE**
>
> **Legal principle**
>
> The court held that there was still a contractual duty to pay rent. This was not discharged by the intervening event of the invasion. The court's view was that liability for intervening events should be covered by express provision for them in the contract.

The courts developed the doctrine of frustration in order to be fairer to parties whose failure to perform was beyond their control. If a contract is frustrated then it ends at the moment that the intervening event prevented performance.

Theories of frustration

There are two main theories behind the doctrine of frustration:

- that there is a new term implied into the contract; or
- that the obligation under the contract has changed.

New implied term

This was considered in *Taylor* v. *Caldwell* (1863) in which Blackburn J stated:

'In contracts which depend on the continued existence of a given person or thing, a condition is implied that the impossibility of performance arising from the perishing of the person or thing shall excuse the performance ... That excuse is by law implied, because from the nature of the contract it is apparent that the parties contracted on the basis of the continued existence of the particular person or chattel.'

Change in the contractual obligation

The implied term theory was criticised for its artificiality. The theory which is now generally preferred is that propounded in *Davis Contractors Ltd* v. *Fareham UDC* (1958). Here Lord Radcliffe set out the test for frustration as follows:

'... there must be a change in the significance of the obligation that the thing undertaken would, if performed, be a different thing than that contracted for'.

EXAM TIP

An understanding of the theory behind a legal principle can make a valuable contribution to essays on a particular topic so it is worth taking time to ensure that you have grasped these different theoretical perspectives on frustration. Remember, though, that such a discussion is appropriate only in an essay and has no place in a problem question.

Types of frustrating event

There are three main classes of situation in which a contract might become frustrated:

■ impossibility
■ illegality
■ change in circumstances.

Impossibility

There are a number of events which can lead to a situation in which it is impossible to perform a contract:

Event	Case
The subject matter of the contract is destroyed	*Taylor* v. *Caldwell* (1863)
The subject matter of the contract becomes unavailable	*Jackson* v. *Union Marine Insurance Co. Ltd* (1874)
A person required for the performance of the contract becomes unavailable through illness	*Robinson* v. *Davidson* (1871)
A person required for the performance of the contract becomes unavailable for other good reason	*Morgan* v. *Manser* (1948)
There is an unavoidable excessive delay	*Pioneer Shipping Ltd* v. *BTP Tioxide Ltd (The Nema)* (1981)

Illegality

A contract may also become frustrated if there is a change in the law that makes the contract illegal to perform in the way that was anticipated in the contract. The courts do not expect parties to be contractually bound to do something illegal. The main cases here arose in wartime when laws are subject to change (such as the requisitioning of goods) to meet unusual circumstances: *Denny, Mott & Dickson Ltd v. James B. Fraser & Co. Ltd* (1944) concerned the commercial sale of timber which was needed for the war effort; *Shipton Anderson & Co. v. Harrison Bros & Co.* (1915) concerned the requisitioning of grain.

Change in circumstances

Contracts may also be frustrated where there is an event which destroys the central purpose of the contract such that all its commercial purpose is destroyed.

KEY CASE

Krell v. *Henry* [1903] 2 KB 740

Concerning: frustration; frustration of purpose

Facts

Henry hired a room from Krell for two days in order to view the coronation procession of Edward VII, but the contract itself made no reference to that intended use. The King's illness caused a postponement of the procession. The defendant refused to pay for the room.

Legal principle

The court held that the contract was frustrated. Henry was excused from paying the rent for the room. The holding of the procession on the dates planned was regarded as the foundation of the contract.

For the contract to be frustrated in this way, all commercial purpose must have been destroyed. If there is some purpose to be found in the contract then it will continue. An example of this can be found in another case which came about from Edward VII's postponed coronation:

KEY CASE

Herne Bay Steamboat Co. v. *Hutton* [1903] 2 KB 683

Concerning: frustration; frustration of purpose

Facts

The defendant hired a boat to sail around the Solent to see the new King's inspection of the fleet that was gathered in port and to see the fleet itself, which was seldom gathered in one place. The inspection was postponed.

KEY CASE

Legal principle

The court held that the contract was not frustrated. Although one purpose (seeing the King's inspection of the fleet) had been destroyed, the defendant was still able to use the boat and see the fleet. The court considered that there was still some commercial value in the contract.

This also applies to leases (*National Carriers Ltd* v. *Panalpina (Northern) Ltd* (1981)) where the purpose of the lease as foreseen by both parties has become impossible and there is therefore no purpose left in the lease.

Limitations on the doctrine of frustration

Although the courts developed the doctrine of frustration to mitigate the harshness from the strict common law position in *Paradine* v. *Jane*, it might still lead to unfair results. The courts have therefore identified certain situations in which the doctrine of frustration does *not* apply:

Situation	Case
The frustration is self-induced	*J. Lauritzen AS* v. *Wijsmuller BV (The Super Servant Two)* (1990)
The contract has merely become more difficult to perform or less beneficial to one of the parties	*Davis Contractors Ltd* v. *Fareham UDC* (1958)
The frustrating event was in the contemplation of the parties at the time that the contract was formed (or the parties should have contemplated that it might occur)	*Amalgamated Investment & Property Co. Ltd* v. *John Walker & Sons Ltd* (1977)
There were provisions in the contract for the frustrating event which covered the extent of the loss or damage caused	*Fibrosa Spolka Akcyjna* v. *Fairbairn Lawson Combe Barbour Ltd* (1943)
The contract expressly provides that performance should occur under any circumstances	*Paradine* v. *Jane* (1647)

The effect of frustration at common law

At common law, the contract ends at the actual point at which it is frustrated – that is, from the frustrating event. Therefore the parties are released from any contractual obligations from that point forward. However, they are still bound by any obligations that arose before the contract was frustrated (see Figure 8.1).

Figure 8.1

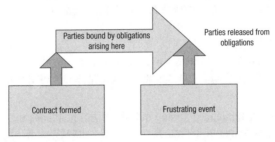

However, this can lead to unfairness. The outcome of frustration of a contract would depend entirely on the point in the contract at which frustration took place. This can be illustrated by yet another case arising from the delayed coronation of Edward VII:

KEY CASE

Chandler v. *Webster* [1904] 1 KB 493

Concerning: frustration; strict common law rule

Facts

As in *Krell* v. *Henry*, the claimant rented a hotel room from the defendant to watch the coronation of King Edward VII. He paid a deposit and agreed to pay the balance on the day. After the cancellation of the coronation, the claimant argued that the contract was frustrated, and claimed the return of his deposit.

Legal principle

As in *Krell* v. *Henry*, the court held that the contract was frustrated. However, the crucial difference here is that the room was paid in advance (*before* the frustrating event), whereas in *Krell* v. *Henry* it was to be paid on the day of the coronation procession. The court therefore would not allow the claimant to recover the money already paid.

The House of Lords modified this position in an attempt to mitigate the harshness of the strict common law rule:

Fibrosa Spolka Akcyjna v. Fairbairn Lawson Combe Barbour Ltd [1943] AC 32

Concerning: frustration; modified common law rule

Facts

A contract for manufacture and delivery of machinery to a Polish company was frustrated by the invasion of Poland which precipitated the Second World War. The Polish company had made a contractual advance payment of £1,000.

Legal principle

The House of Lords held that a party *could* recover payments made prior to a frustrating event, provided that there was a total failure of consideration. Per Lord Macmillan:

> 'Owing to circumstances arising out of present hostilities the contract has become impossible of fulfilment according to its terms. Neither party is to blame. In return for their money the plaintiffs [now claimants] have received nothing whatever from the defendants by way of fulfilment of any part of the contract. It is thus a typical case of a total failure of consideration. The money paid must be repaid.'

This is an improvement over the position from *Chandler* v. *Webster* (1904). However, it is still not ideal: for instance, in *Fibrosa* the manufacturer received no payment for any work that it had done in advance of the contract. As a result, Parliament, following *Fibrosa*, intervened with statute in the form of the Law Reform (Frustrated Contracts) Act 1943.

The Law Reform (Frustrated Contracts) Act 1943

The Act deals with three areas:

- recovery of *money paid in advance*
- recovery of *work already completed*
- recovery for a *benefit gained through partial performance*.

Money paid in advance

Law Reform (Frustrated Contracts) Act 1943, section 1(2)

'All sums paid or payable to any party in pursuance of the contract before the time when the parties were so discharged (in this Act referred to as 'the time

KEY STATUTE

of discharge') shall, in the case of sums so paid, be recoverable from him as money received by him for the use of the party by whom the sums were paid, and, in the case of sums so payable, cease to be so payable:

Provided that, if the party to whom the sums were so paid or payable incurred expenses before the time of discharge in, or for the purpose of, the performance of the contract, the court may, if it considers it just to do so having regard to all the circumstances of the case, allow him to retain or, as the case may be, recover the whole or any part of the sums so paid or payable, not being an amount in excess of the expenses so incurred.'

This provision confirms the *Fibrosa* principle that money already paid is recoverable and that money due under the contract ceases to be payable (as in *Taylor* v. *Caldwell* (1863)).

Work already completed

Under section 1(2) the court also has discretion to reward a party who has already carried out work under or in preparation for the contract. However, this is discretionary and therefore does not automatically guarantee that all actual expenses will be recoverable (*Gamerco SA* v. *ICM/Fair Warning Agency* (1995)).

Benefit gained through partial performance

Section 1(3) of the Act considers recovery for partial performance:

KEY STATUTE

Law Reform (Frustrated Contracts) Act 1943, section 1(3)

'Where any party to the contract has, by reason of anything done by any other party thereto in, or for the purpose of, the performance of the contract, obtained a valuable benefit (other than a payment of money to which the last foregoing subsection applies) before the time of discharge, there shall be recoverable from him by the said other party such sum (if any), not exceeding the value of the said benefit to the party obtaining it, as the court considers just, having regard to all the circumstances of the case and, in particular, –

(a) the amount of any expenses incurred before the time of discharge by the benefited party in, or for the purpose of, the performance of the contract, including any sums paid or payable by him to any other party in pursuance of the contract and retained or recoverable by that party under the last foregoing subsection, and

(b) the effect, in relation to the said benefit, of the circumstances giving rise to the frustration of the contract.'

Therefore, the court must first consider whether a valuable benefit has been conferred. Having established this, the court must consider a just sum to award in all the circumstances. In essence, this discretion exists to prevent unjust enrichment of one of the parties (*BP Exploration Co. (Libya) Ltd* v. *Hunt (No. 2)* (1979)).

Restrictions on the Act

The Act specifically excludes certain circumstances:

Circumstance	Section
The contract is severable and one part has been completely performed. The court treats the severable part as though it were separate.	2(4)
Carriage of goods by sea (except time charter-parties)	2(5)(a)
Contracts of insurance	2(5)(b)
Perishing of goods under section 7 of the Sale of Goods Act 1979	2(5)(c)

Chapter Summary:
Putting it all together

TEST YOURSELF

☐ Can you tick all the points from the revision checklist at the beginning of this chapter?

☐ Take the **end-of-chapter quiz** on the Companion Website.

☐ Test your knowledge of the cases below with the **revision flashcards** on the website.

☐ Attempt the essay question from the beginning of the chapter using the guidelines below.

☐ Go to the Companion Website to try out other questions.

Answer guidelines

See the essay question at the start of the chapter.

Points to remember when answering this question:

▪ You need to provide a strong introduction which 'unpicks' the statement by Bingham LJ, identifies the key issues within it and sets out the approach the remainder of your answer is going to take.

▪ Consider the underlying object: to achieve a fair result. Therefore you should demonstrate how the law was unfair in the first place: absolute obligations under *Paradine* v. *Jane*.

▪ Explain the three main ways in which a contract may become frustrated: impossibility, illegality, change in circumstances. Provide examples from case law of each that would demonstrate unfairness if the doctrine did not exist.

▪ You should then point out that the doctrine may still lead to unfair results, and show how the courts developed certain situations in which it does *not* apply – with examples from case law.

▪ Explain how the effect of frustration at common law can also lead to unfair outcomes – the parties originally being bound by obligations prior to frustration (*Chandler* v. *Webster*) and how this led to the modification in *Fibrosa* and ultimately the enactment of the Law Reform (Frustrated Contracts) Act 1943.

▪ Describe the areas that the Act covers and its restrictions. Consider whether there are still situations in which the outcome of frustration may lead to unfairness.

▪ Finally you should draw all the strands of your argument together in a cohesive and coherent conclusion that addresses the quotation directly and provides a focused answer to the question.

Make your answer really stand out:

▪ It is important in an essay such as this to maintain focus on the question. Ask yourself at the end of each paragraph whether the points you have made relate to the question. If not, see if there is anything that you could use to draw reference to the quotation. Otherwise you run the risk of being overly descriptive and will lose marks available for analysis.

▪ There are many examples derived from case law in this area so it is important to illustrate the points you make with cases. If you can use the facts of the cases to demonstrate unfairness (or mitigation of unfairness) this will show greater understanding of the requirements of the question.

▪ Remember that there are restrictions on the Law Reform (Frustrated Contracts) Act 1943 provided in section 2. These are often overlooked.

9
Remedies

A printable version of this topic map is available from www.pearsoned.co.uk/lawexpress

Revision Checklist

What you need to know:

☐ The circumstances in which the availability of damages is limited: causation, remoteness and the duty to mitigate

☐ The distinction between methods of calculating damages: loss of bargain and reliance loss

☐ How special categories of damages, such as loss of amenity, mental distress and loss of a chance, are assessed

☐ The circumstances in which specific performance is available as a remedy for breach of contract.

Introduction:
Remedies

Although you will often be asked whether a party can 'enforce the contract', the most usual remedy is not specific performance, which would compel the party in breach to fulfil their contractual obligations, but damages.

Damages are a common law remedy and are available as of right if there has been a breach of contract. This chapter will explore the limitations on the availability of damages – issues of causation and remoteness and the duty to mitigate loss – as well as looking at methods for calculating damages. It will also consider the tricky issue of damages that cover non-pecuniary loss. These issues are important as you need to be able to assess not only whether there is a claim for breach of contract but also what the innocent party is likely to receive as a result of that breach. The chapter will move on to consider specific performance. As this is an equitable remedy, it is available at the discretion of the court so it is important that you are able to identify the circumstances in which the courts will compel the party in breach to continue with the performance of the contract.

Essay question advice

Essays on remedies are not popular with students although they do appear on exam papers quite frequently. Such questions may specify that they are looking for a discussion of damages, e.g. 'discuss the extent to which an award of damages is an adequate remedy for breach of contract', or they may be phrased more generally, e.g. 'assess what remedies are available to a party who has suffered breach of contract'. Make sure you have sufficient knowledge to undertake the analysis required by the essay before deciding to answer it. For example, it would be unwise to attempt a question asking about the adequacy of damages as a remedy for breach of contract if you could describe only the method of calculating damages without any notion of the issues to raise when discussing whether they are always an adequate remedy.

Problem question advice

Problem questions on damages will often combine with some other topic as they are a remedy for breach of contract, so the facts will need to establish a cause of action for the claimant in order for them to be awarded a remedy. It is important to read the instructions carefully to see what the question requires: if you are asked to 'consider whether Tess can recover damages' then there is no need to do anything more than this as no credit would be available for considering contract formation and breach. However, if the question stipulated 'consider whether there is a valid contract, whether it has been breached and what remedies are available to Tess' then formation and breach would be relevant in addition to a consideration of remedies.

Sample question

Could you answer this question? Below is a typical problem question that could arise on this topic. Guidelines on answering the question are included at the end of the chapter, whilst a sample essay question and guidance on tackling it can be found on the Companion Website.

Problem question

Sally has been made redundant from her job as a university lecturer. She enjoys cooking so decides to use her redundancy payment to start her own catering business. She enters into a contract with Alan which stipulates that he will convert her garage into a large kitchen and install commercial catering equipment. The contract specifies that the work must be completed within four weeks. Alan commences work and Sally sets about generating interest in her new business. She spends £5,000 on promotional literature and advertising and she is pleased to receive a booking to cater for a silver wedding anniversary in five weeks' time. Sally tells Alan about the booking and checks to ensure that the work will be finished in time and Alan assures her that he is ahead of schedule. Sally receives an enquiry from a local business about the provision of executive lunches for 12 people every weekday and enters into negotiations to secure this contract. Three days prior to the date agreed for completion of the kitchen, Alan admits to Sally that the work is hopelessly behind schedule and that it is likely to take him another four weeks to complete the kitchen. Sally has to cancel the anniversary booking. News of this reaches the local business and they contact Sally to tell her that they have no interest in engaging her services because she is unreliable. Sally has a breakdown due to the stress caused by the failure of her business.

Advise Sally as to the extent of her claim in damages against Alan.

Damages

KEY DEFINITION

Damages are a financial remedy that aims to compensate the injured party for the consequences of the breach of contract. In general, the principle that guides the award of damages is that the injured party should be put into the position, as far as is possible, that they would have been in if the contract had been carried out.

The aim of an award of damages is to ensure that the innocent party does not suffer as a result of the other party's breach of contract but is put in the same position that they would have been in had the other party honoured their contractual obligations. It is important to remember that contractual damages are restorative not punitive, per Lord Atkinson in *Addis* v. *Gramophone Co. Ltd* (1909):

'I have always understood that damages for breach of contract were in the nature of compensation, not punishment.'

Limitations on the availability of damages

It might seem logical to expect that an innocent party that can establish that the other contracting party has breached the contract would be able to claim damages but there are three factors to take into account that may limit the availability of damages:

▌ causation
▌ remoteness
▌ mitigation of loss.

Causation

A claimant can only recover damages if the breach of contract caused his loss. It is not enough that there is breach of contract and loss: the loss must be a consequence of the breach. As such, an intervening act that occurs between the breach of contract and the loss may breach the chain of causation (see Figure 9.1).

KEY CASE

County Ltd v. *Girozentrale Securities* [1996] 3 All ER 834

Concerning: chain of causation, intervening acts

Facts

The claimant bank underwrote the issue of 26 million shares in an oil exploration company. The defendant was a firm of stockbrokers engaged by the claimant to find investors interested in the shares. The defendant set about finding investors but acted outside of the terms of their agreement with the claimant and, as a result of this and other factors, many of the shares were unsold. The claimant brought an action to recover the loss, which was in the region of £7 million.

Legal principle

The Court of Appeal upheld the claimant's appeal on the basis that the defendant had acted outside of their instructions and that this breach of contract was an effective cause of the claimant's loss. It was immaterial that other factors, including the claimant's own conduct, contributed to the loss.

As such, it is clear that the breach of conduct may be *a* cause of the loss, i.e. one of several causes, rather than *the* cause, i.e. the sole cause of loss.

EXAM TIP

It is important that you remember to mention causation in your answer to a problem question on this topic. Even though the issue of causation is not usually complicated when it arises in a problem question, many students omit to mention it at all. It is important to cover causation so that your answer is complete and so that you can attract marks for dealing with this often-forgotten issue.

Figure 9.1

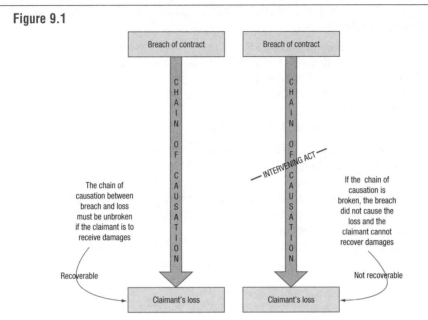

Remoteness

Causation is the first hurdle that must be cleared in order for the injured party to recover damages from the party in breach but, having done this, it is then necessary to establish that the loss, even though caused by the breach, was not too remote from it. In other words, not all loss that is caused by breach of contract is recoverable.

Hadley v. *Baxendale* (1854) 9 Ex 341

Concerning: damages and remoteness

Facts

The claimants owned a mill. A crankshaft, which was essential for the operation of the mill, broke and needed to be replaced using the original as a template. The claimants engaged the defendants, a firm of carriers, to transport the broken part to engineers in Greenwich where a replacement would be made but the defendants failed to do this within the timeframe specified thus delaying the arrival of the new part and causing the mill to stand inoperative. The claimants sought damages to compensate for the losses sustained whilst the mill was idle.

KEY CASE

Legal principle

The Court of Exchequer accepted the defendants' submission that the loss was too remote and should not be recoverable. It would have been an entirely different position if the defendants had been made aware that the mill would be inoperable without the part but they were not aware that this was the only crankshaft that the claimant possessed.

This judgment gave rise to the foreseeability test (per Alderson B):

'Where two parties have made a contract which one of them has broken, the damages which the other party ought to receive in respect of such breach of contract should be such as may fairly and reasonably be considered either arising naturally, i.e., according to the usual course of things, from such breach of contract itself, or such as may reasonably be supposed to have been in the contemplation of both parties at the time they made the contract as the probable result of the breach of it.'

This creates two situations in which the requirements of remoteness will be satisfied that are referred to as the two limbs of the *Hadley* v. *Baxendale* test of foreseeability (see Figure 9.2).

Figure 9.2

The *Hadley* v. *Baxendale* principle was considered in two subsequent cases:

KEY CASES

Victoria Laundry Ltd v. *Newman Industries* [1949] 2 KB 528

Concerning: remoteness, loss within the contemplation of the parties

Facts

The claimants ran a laundry business. They purchased a boiler from the defendants that was due for delivery in July. The boiler sustained some damage and had to be repaired which delayed delivery until November. The claimants had made the defendants aware that they needed the boiler to expand their business and that they wanted it for immediate use. They claimed damages to represent the loss of ordinary profits that would have been made from their additional business if the boiler had arrived as agreed and also for the loss of government contracts that they had intended to secure once the boiler arrived.

Legal principle

It was held that the claimants could recover damages for the loss of additional profit but not for the loss of revenue from the government contracts. This was because the defendants were aware that the claimants aimed to increase their business by acquiring another boiler, thus the loss of the additional income was a 'reasonably foreseeable' consequence of breach, whereas there was nothing to suggest that the defendants were aware of the claimants' plans concerning government contracts so this was not recoverable.

Victoria Laundry provides an example of the operation of the second limb and sets the standard of remoteness as 'reasonable foreseeability' but the House of Lords disagreed with this level of probability in *The Heron II*:

The Heron II [1969] 1 AC 350

Concerning: remoteness, loss within the contemplation of the parties

Facts

The claimant chartered *The Heron II* to transport a cargo of sugar on a journey that should have taken 20 days but actually, due to a deviation from the route by the defendant, took 29 days during which the price of sugar fell significantly. The late arrival put the defendant in breach of contract so the claimant sought damages to cover the difference in the price he received for the sugar and the higher price that he would have received had the boat arrived on time. The claimant had not told the defendant that he intended to sell the sugar at the destination but the defendant was aware that he was carrying sugar and that the destination was a popular trading place for sugar.

Legal principle

The House of Lords held that, although the claimant had not told the defendant that he intended to sell the sugar as soon as the boat arrived, the defendant's knowledge that he was carrying sugar and his awareness that the destination was a popular trading place for sugar was sufficient to make it so probable that it must have been within his contemplation at the time the contract was made. The House of Lords criticised the reference to 'reasonable foresight' in *Victoria Laundry*, as this is a term that is more appropriate in tort, with Lord Reid stating:

> 'The question for decision is whether a [claimant] can recover as damages for breach of contract a loss of the kind which the defendant, when he made the contract, ought to have realised was not unlikely to result from a breach of contract . . . I use the words "not unlikely" as denoting a degree of probability considerably less than an even chance but nevertheless not very unusual and easily foreseeable.'

EXAM TIP

Remember that if you are dealing with this issue in a problem question, you will need to state the legal principle established in *Hadley* v. *Baxendale* and refer to examples of the rule in operation in cases such as *Victoria Laundry* or *The Heron II*. However, if you were revising this topic in preparation for an essay question, you would need a more detailed understanding of the judicial reasoning in each of these cases plus the ability to engage in critical comment of the way in which the law has developed. You might find it useful to read an article which discusses remoteness and its treatment in case law such as Tettenborn, A., '*Hadley* v. *Baxendale* Foreseeability: a Principle Beyond its Sell-by Date?' (2003) *Journal of Contract Law* 120 to give you some ideas for critical analysis in an essay.

Mitigation of loss

The third factor to take into account when considering the availability and quantification of damages is the duty to mitigate.

KEY DEFINITION

The **duty to mitigate** refers to a principle of contract law whereby the innocent party who has suffered a breach of contract has a duty to take reasonable steps to minimise the extent of their loss arising from the breach.

The innocent victim of a breach of contract will be entitled to damages to cover losses caused by the breach that are not too remote provided he has not failed to take action that would have reduced the extent of his losses.

Brace v. *Calder* [1895] 2 QB 253

Concerning: duty to take reasonable steps to mitigate loss

Facts

The claimant was offered employment for a period of two years. After five months, the company was dissolved due to the retirement of two of its owners which cut short the claimant's employment. However, two of the owners continued the business in their own right and offered the claimant employment which he refused.

Legal principle

His claim for damages to cover the loss of earnings for the remainder of the two-year period was refused on the basis that he had failed to take advantage of the opportunity to reduce his losses by accepting the offer of employment.

The key point to remember here is to think about what it was reasonable for the claimant to do in the circumstances to reduce the extent of their losses. This will depend on the factual circumstances involved in each situation. Note that it is only required that the claimant takes reasonable steps to minimise his losses – the courts have held that a claimant should not be expected to take onerous measures to limit their loss.

Pilkington v. *Wood* [1953] 2 All ER 810

Concerning: duty to take reasonable steps to mitigate loss

Facts

The claimant bought a house but there was a defect in the title that meant that he was not able to take possession of the property for some time whilst the situation was rectified. The claimant's solicitor was in breach of contract for his failure to take appropriate steps to spot the defect in title; thus the claimant brought an action to recover damages relating to the costs of hotel bills and many other costs associated with the delay in the completion of the sale. The defendant solicitor argued that the claimant could have pursued the vendor of the property for these costs and that this would have been a reasonable measure to take to mitigate the losses arising from the solicitor's breach of contract.

Legal principle

The defendant's argument was rejected. A claim against the vendor would have required the claimant to pursue complicated litigation which may not have been successful whereas the breach of contract claim against the solicitor was straightforward. As such, it was not reasonable to expect the claimant to take the risk of pursuing the vendor so there was no duty to do so in order to mitigate the losses arising from the solicitor's breach of contract.

Calculation of damages

As damages are available as of right, the question is not whether the successful claimant will receive damages (they will subject to issues of causation, remoteness and mitigation) but how the amount of damages payable is to be calculated. There are two methods of determining the extent of damages that will be awarded:

- *loss of a bargain*: places the innocent party in the position they would have been in if the contract had been performed.
- *reliance loss*: places the innocent party in the position they would have been in if the contract had never been made.

Each of these will be considered in more detail in the sections that follow.

Before doing so, it is important to note that, as the aim of damages is either to place the innocent party in the position they would have been in if the contract had been performed (loss of bargain) or if the contract had never been made (reliance loss), a defendant who has neither spent nor lost money cannot recover damages. For example, if Tom agrees to sell his car to Chris but Chris changes his mind and refuses to pay, he is in breach of contract. If Tom is able to sell the car for the same or higher price to James, Tom has lost nothing as a result of Chris's breach so would receive only *nominal damages*, i.e. a small sum to acknowledge the breach of contract.

Loss of a bargain

This is the main category of damages awarded for breach of contract. It is sometimes known as 'expectation loss' as the innocent party has lost what he expected to receive from the contract. As such, this form of damages aims to put the innocent party in the position that they would have been in if the contract had been performed.

There are two possible situations:

1. There is no performance by one of the parties to the contract. This could mean that the party who was bound to supply goods or services failed to do so or it could mean that the party who was due to receive goods or services refused to accept them. In this case, damages will represent the cost to the innocent party of

obtaining the goods or services that should have been supplied. This may be the actual value of the contract if a substitute can be found at that price or at the market value of the goods/services which may be higher than the price agreed in the contract.

Substitute at actual value: *Charter* v. *Sullivan* (1957)	Substitute at market value: *WL Thompson Ltd* v. *Robinson Gunmakers Ltd* (1955)

In both of these cases, the defendant had agreed to purchase a car but subsequently refused to complete the transaction thus putting himself in breach of contract.

The claimant accepted that there was a good market for the car thus it would not be difficult to obtain the same price from another purchaser. As such, they had suffered no loss so only nominal damages were awarded.	Here, there was less demand for the car in question and it was likely that it would be sold for a lower price than that agreed with the defendant. As such, the claimant was entitled to damages to reflect the loss of profit.

2. There is performance in the sense that goods or services are provided but these are defective or of an inferior quality to that stipulated by the contract. Here, damages will either cover the cost of restoring the goods to the expected quality (cost of cure) or represent the gap in the price between the goods expected (good quality/undamaged) and those received (inferior quality/defective) (difference in value). This may also raise issues of whether it is the actual value or market value that is the appropriate basis for calculation of damages.

KEY CASE

Ruxley Electronics and Construction Ltd v. *Forsyth* [1995] 3 WLR 118

Concerning: basis for calculating damages

Facts

The claimant engaged the services of the defendant to construct a swimming pool at a cost of £70,000. When it was completed, the depth of the pool was several inches less than had been stipulated in the contract. The cost of rectifying the defect by rebuilding the swimming pool would have been over £20,000 (cost of cure) which would have imposed an unacceptable hardship on the defendant, given that the pool was perfectly functional in every other respect. The difference in depth made no difference to the value of the pool so the claimant received only nominal damages (although an award of £2,500 was made for loss of amenity).

▶

Legal principle

The House of Lords emphasised that the aim of damages was to put the innocent party in the position they would have been in if the contract had been performed but ruled that this did not necessarily mean that the innocent party would be entitled to the monetary equivalent of specific performance.

Reliance loss

There are situations in which it is difficult or impossible to calculate damages on the basis of the position that the defendant would have been in if the contract had been performed so a different basis for calculation is used that focuses on loss caused by reliance on the contract. Here, the aim is to place the innocent party in the position that they would have been in if the contract had never been made.

Anglia Television Ltd v. *Reed* [1972] 1 QB 60

Concerning: calculation of reliance loss

Facts

The claimant television company entered into a contract with the actor, Robert Reed, to star in a film. Reed subsequently decided to take part in an American film and, as the filming would have clashed with the claimant's film, refused to go ahead thus breaching his contract. As a result, the film was abandoned. The claimant sought to recover expenditure both before and after the contract was signed on the basis that this money was spent in reliance on the contract with the defendant.

Legal principle

It was uncomplicated to find that expenditure after the contract was formed was recoverable as it was reasonable to expect that the film company would spend money preparing for filming. It was less clear that damages were recoverable for expenditure incurred prior to the formation of the contract as it seemed less clear that these arose due to reliance on the contract as the contract did not exist at the time. However, it was held that there was no reason why costs incurred prior to the contract could not be recoverable provided that they were not too remote. As the defendant was aware that all costs associated with making the film would be wasted if the contract did not go ahead, the claimant was able to claim damages for money spent prior to the formation of the contract.

In *Anglia Television Ltd* v. *Reed*, the Court of Appeal also stated that it was for the claimant to decide whether they wanted to claim for expectation loss or reliance loss.

Reliance loss provides a good basis for a claim of damages for claimants who cannot establish what, if anything, they have lost that falls within expectation loss. Here, for example, the film company did not seek damages for expectation loss based upon the profit that the film would have made as this would have been too difficult to predict.

Non-pecuniary loss

Damages are an award of a sum of money that aims to put the innocent party in the position they would have been in if the contract had been performed (expectation loss) or not made (reliance loss) so it follows that the calculation of damages is most straightforward in relation to financial loss. For many years, damages were limited to pecuniary loss but it is now recognised that there are situations in which damages may be paid in relation to injury to feelings, mental distress and loss of amenity.

KEY CASE

Jarvis v. *Swans Tours* [1973] 1 All ER 71

Concerning: damages for loss of enjoyment

Facts

The claimant booked a two-week holiday that specified certain features, such as a welcome party, afternoon tea and yodelling sessions. These features were either absent (the welcome party) or unsatisfactory (afternoon tea and yodelling). The holiday company was clearly in breach of contract for failing to provide these features but the issue was the extent to which the claimant could recover for their absence given that they amounted to loss of enjoyment rather than financial loss.

Legal principle

At first instance, the claimant recovered only a small sum to cover the cost of the features that he had not received but, on appeal, his award was increased to reflect damages for the loss of enjoyment. The rationale for the decision was that the very purpose of a holiday is enjoyment therefore it followed that damages should be available if the level of enjoyment promised was not forthcoming.

This notion of identifying the very object or purpose of the contract and providing damages if that object is not provided also enables claimants to recover for the mental distress associated with the failure of the contract. This is applicable only to contracts where the essence of the contract is to provide pleasure: there can be no recovery for mental distress in purely commercial contracts.

Cases in which damages have been awarded for mental distress include:

- a sum awarded to represent the disappointment and anxiety caused by the non-appearance of a wedding photographer: *Diesen* v. *Sampson* (1971);
- damages for mental distress arising from a solicitor's negligent failure to obtain an injunction to protect the claimant from molestation: *Heywood* v. *Wellers* (1976).

Damages may be awarded for loss of amenity as was the case in *Ruxley Electronics and Construction Ltd* v. *Forsyth* (discussed above).

There are situations in which damages may be available in relation to the loss of chance caused by breach of contract:

- In *Blackpool and Fylde Aero Club* v. *Blackpool Borough Council* (1990) damages were awarded to the claimant when Blackpool Borough Council failed to consider their application for a tender, as this had deprived them of the chance to win the contract, even though it was by no means certain that they would have done so.
- In *Chaplin* v. *Hicks* (1911), the claimant received damages to represent the lost chance of success in a beauty contest even though her success was only a possibility not a certainty.

Action for an agreed sum

If the price to be paid for performance of the contract is specified but payment is not forthcoming once performance has taken place, the innocent party may bring an action for an agreed sum. This is not the same as damages as the innocent party is seeking to enforce the contract by compelling the other party to pay rather than seeking compensation for loss suffered. The time at which payment is due will depend on the terms of the contract.

An action for an agreed sum is straightforward where a price is specified as there is no issue of remoteness and no need for quantification of damages. Difficulties arise if a price is not specified but there has been some performance of the contractual obligation. In such a situation, the price is calculated on a *quantum meruit* basis: that is, as much money as is deserved in relation to the work done. This is calculated on the basis of the market price for the work in question.

■ Specific performance

KEY DEFINITION

Specific performance is an equitable remedy that compels the party in breach to perform his part of the contract. It is generally positive in nature, i.e. it compels

▶

the party in breach to do something, as opposed to an injunction which is negative or prohibitory in nature, i.e. it compels a person to refrain from doing something.

It is important to remember that damages are the main remedy for breach of contract. Damages are available as of right, i.e. once breach of contract is established, the injured party is entitled to an award of damages, whereas the availability of specific performance is limited on the basis of three considerations, each of which will be considered in turn:

▌ It is only available if damages are not an adequate remedy.
▌ As it is an equitable remedy, it is available at the discretion of the judge.
▌ It is only available for certain types of contract.

Damages are not an adequate remedy

Specific performance is only available if damages are not an adequate remedy and it is for the claimant to establish that this is the case.

No substitute is available

The essence of breach of contract is that one party has failed to provide that which he was bound to provide. An award of damages will often enable the claimant to purchase that property or service from an alternative source; in other words, the party in breach will pay the injured party a sufficient sum to enable him to pay someone else to do that which the party in breach should have done. However, if there is no alternative source available – such as the purchase of 'one-off' goods – then damages are not adequate as no amount of money can purchase something which is simply not available.

KEY CASE

Cohen v. *Roche* [1927] 1 KB 169

Concerning: availability of substitute goods

Facts

The claimant purchased eight Hepplewhite chairs at auction but the defendant refused to honour the sale as he claimed that there had been some irregularity in the transaction. The court held that the sale was valid but ordered an award of damages rather than the order of specific performance sought by the claimant.

Legal principle

It was held that the chairs were 'unremarkable' and possessed no special feature that made them unique and irreplaceable. As such, the claimant could obtain substitute chairs from another source and an order of specific performance would not be appropriate.

KEY CASE

Phillips v. *Lamdin* [1949] 2 KB 33

Concerning: unavailability of substitute goods

Facts

The claimant agreed to purchase a house from the defendant which included a rare ornate door made by Adam. The defendant delayed the sale of the house and removed the door prior to the completion of the sale.

Legal principle

It was held that the door could not be remade or refashioned – 'you cannot make a new Adam door' – thus it was not an option for the defendant to offer money to cover the value of the door but he must return it to its original position in the house.

The key feature to look out for here is whether the property in question is, if not entirely unique, of limited availability as only then is it possible that an order of specific performance will be made to compel the party in breach to deliver the goods. Remember that the courts tend to view land as unique irrespective of its characteristics.

An award of damages would be unfair to the claimant

An award of damages would not be adequate if it would cause unfairness to the claimant, i.e. it would leave the claimant without adequate recompense. For example, if the financial value of the loss is very low, a successful claimant will receive only nominal damages, so this would not be an appropriate way of dealing with the case.

KEY CASE

Beswick v. *Beswick* [1968] AC 58

Concerning: unfairness to the claimant

Facts

The claimant was the widow of a coal merchant who, prior to his death, had sold the goodwill in his business to the defendant on the agreement that the

KEY CASE

defendant would pay an annuity to the coal merchant during his lifetime and to his widow after his death. The defendant made one payment to the coal merchant and none to his widow. The claimant was not a party to the contract and so she could not sue for the unpaid annuity; instead she brought an action on behalf of her deceased husband's estate.

Legal principle

It would be unfair to the claimant to award damages as a remedy as these would only be nominal because the estate had suffered no loss as a result of the breach of contract, whereas an order of specific performance would compel the defendant to pay the unpaid sums and to continue to pay the annuity in the future.

Sale of Goods Act 1979, section 52

KEY STATUTE

Sale of Goods Act 1979, section 52(1)

'In any action for breach of contract to deliver specific or ascertained goods the court may, if it thinks fit, on the plaintiff's [now claimant's] application, by its judgment or decree direct that the contract shall be performed specifically, without giving the defendant the option of retaining the goods on payment of damages.'

This means that, if the goods are specific or ascertained, specific performance is available at the court's discretion. Despite this, in practice, the courts apply the common law 'availability of a substitute' rule to determine whether specific performance should be awarded.

Discretion of the court

As it is an equitable remedy, specific performance will only be ordered in accordance with the rules of equity; it was held in *Stickney* v. *Keeble* (1915) that 'equity will only grant specific performance if, under all the circumstances, it is just and equitable to do so'. An examination of case law identifies a number of principles that have been developed which guide the exercise of this discretion:

- A claimant who delays in bringing an action may be denied specific performance: *Milward* v. *Earl of Thanet* (1801) (delay defeats equity).
- Specific performance is not available to a claimant who has behaved dishonestly or improperly: *Walters* v. *Morgan* (1861) (he who comes to equity must come with clean hands).

- A defendant may resist specific performance on the basis that it would cause extreme hardship to him: *Patel* v. *Ali* (1984).
- Specific performance will be refused if it is not possible for the defendant to perform what was agreed, i.e. if the property no longer belongs to the defendant.
- A claimant will not be granted specific performance where he has provided no consideration (equity will not assist a volunteer).
- Specific performance will only be granted if the claimant is also willing to perform his side of the bargain.
- Specific performance will not be ordered if the contract requires performance over a period of time so that constant supervision is needed as this would be impractical: *Co-operative Insurance Society Ltd* v. *Argyll Stores (Holdings) Ltd* (1997) (equity does nothing in vain).

KEY CASE

Co-operative Insurance Society Ltd v. Argyll Stores (Holdings) Ltd [1997] 3 All ER 297

Concerning: constant supervision

Facts

The defendants operated a supermarket in a large unit that they leased in the claimants' retail centre. The lease had a covenant that required the supermarket to be open during normal business hours but it became unprofitable for the defendants and they ceased trading. The claimants feared that this would have an adverse impact on the level of trade in the retail centre, so they sought an order of specific performance to compel the defendants to reopen the supermarket and resume trading.

Legal principle

The House of Lords, overturning the ruling of the Court of Appeal, held that it was not practical for the courts to force the defendants to carry out their business as it would need constant supervision by the courts to ensure compliance. Moreover, given that the defendants ceased trading for economic reasons, specific performance would place them in the position of either having to trade an unprofitable business or pay damages to the court for contempt if they chose to defy the order of specific performance.

Type of contract

As a general rule, specific performance will not be ordered in relation to contracts for personal services, such as a contract of employment. Section 236 of the Trade Union and Labour Relations (Consolidation) Act 1992 states that it is unlawful to compel an employee to work by means of an order of specific performance or by grant of an injunction. Moreover, although an employment tribunal can order reinstatement or re-engagement of an employee who should not have been dismissed, it is rare for them to do so. There are pragmatic reasons for this position:

> 'Very rarely indeed will a court enforce .., a contract for services. The reason is obvious; if one party has no faith in the honesty, integrity or the loyalty of the other, to force him to serve or employ that other is a plain recipe for disaster.'

> (Per Geoffrey Lane LJ in *Chappell* v. *Times Newspapers Ltd* [1975] 1 WLR 482 at 506.)

FURTHER THINKING

The relationship between damages and specific performance as remedies for breach of contract has been the subject of a fair amount of academic discussion. If you were required to evaluate the desirability of the availability of both remedies as part of an essay, familiarity with the academic debate would be useful. William Bishop's article 'The Choice of Remedy for Breach of Contract' (1985) 14 *Legal Studies* 299 provides a detailed examination of this issue.

Chapter Summary:
Putting it all together

TEST YOURSELF

- [ ] Can you tick all the points from the revision checklist at the beginning of this chapter?
- [ ] Take the **end-of-chapter quiz** on the Companion Website.
- [ ] Test your knowledge of the cases below with the **revision flashcards** on the website.
- [ ] Attempt the problem question from the beginning of the chapter using the guidelines below.
- [ ] Go to the Companion Website to try out other questions.

Answer guidelines

See the problem question at the start of the chapter.

Points to remember when answering this question:

■ Make sure that you pay attention to the instructions that accompany the question. This question does not require any consideration of contract formation or breach as it is specific in its instruction to consider Sally's claim for damages. This means that there are no marks available for discussion of any other topic and should indicate to you that a good depth of knowledge about damages is needed to address this question properly.

■ Start by picking out all of the areas where Sally has lost actual or expected money as these are a good basis for a claim in damages. Once you have located these, see what facts remain and consider whether there is any non-pecuniary loss that could be reflected by an award of damages.

■ Can Sally recover the loss of profit from the anniversary booking? Remember that you must establish that Alan's breach of contract caused the loss and that it is not too remote. Take the *Hadley* v. *Baxendale* limbs into account here: was it in the ordinary course of things or was it within the contemplation of the parties at the time the contract was made? It is likely that Alan was aware that Sally had a booking given the emphasis that was placed on the timing of the completion of the kitchen.

■ Can Sally recover for the loss of the executive lunches booking? Consider causation and remoteness again. Was this within the contemplation of the parties at the time the contract was made? It could be argued that this is analogous to the government contracts in *Victoria Laundry* because Alan could not be expected to be aware of any other plans Sally had for securing bookings but there is a counter-argument that he must have been aware that she would seek some additional bookings.

■ Can Sally recover damages in relation to the mental distress she has suffered following the failure of her business? This is unlikely for two reasons, both of which should be explained in detail. First, *Addis* v. *Gramophone Co. Ltd* provides that damages for mental distress are not available in commercial contracts and both Sally and Alan are acting in a commercial context. Secondly, damages for mental distress have been limited to cases such as *Jarvis* v. *Swans Tours* where the enjoyment was the essential character of the contract.

Make your answer really stand out:

■ A stronger answer to the question will consider whether a claim of damages based on reliance loss or one based on expectation loss (loss of bargain) will be the best course of action for Sally.

■ Always remember to incorporate relevant case law into your answer as this provides support for the legal principles that you have stated.

■ Reach a conclusion that deals with each of the three points and which evaluates the likelihood that Sally will be successful in her claim for damages. If you feel that it is unlikely that she will succeed on a particular issue, make sure that you explain why this is so in your conclusion even though you have already explored this in the main body of your answer.

And finally, before the exam . . .

By using this revision guide to direct your work, you should now have a good knowledge and understanding of the way in which the various aspects of the law of contract law work in isolation and the many ways in which they are interrelated. What's more, you should have acquired the skills and techniques necessary to demonstrate that knowledge and understanding in the examination, regardless of whether the questions are presented to you in essay or problem form.

TEST YOURSELF

- ☐ Look at the summary checklist of the points at the end of the book. Are you happy that you can now tick them all? If not, go back to the particular chapter and work through the material again. If you are still struggling, **seek help** from your tutor.
- ☐ Go to the Companion Website and revisit the interactive **quizzes** provided for each chapter.
- ☐ Make sure you can recall the **legal principles** of the key cases and statutory provisions which you have revised.
- ☐ Go to the Companion Website and test your knowledge of cases and terms with the **revision flashcards.**

Summary checklist

Do you know:

- ▐ The definitions of offer and acceptance?
- ▐ The distinction between an offer, an invitation to treat and a counter-offer?
- ▐ The rules on communication and withdrawal of offers?
- ▐ The rules relating to communication of acceptances?

- The presumptions of legal intent which arise in social, domestic and commercial situations?
- The definition of consideration?
- The rules relating to 'good' consideration?
- The exceptions to the general rule that performance of an existing duty is not good consideration?
- The rules relating to part payment of debts?
- The development and operation of promissory estoppel?
- The operation of the general doctrine of privity of contract?
- The various exceptions to the general rule of privity?
- The circumstances in which a third party to a contract may recover damages?
- The main provisions of the Contracts (Rights of Third Parties) Act 1999 and their effects?
- The remedies that are available to a third party under the Contracts (Rights of Third Parties) Act 1999?
- The distinction between a representation and a term of the contract and the consequences of the distinction?
- The difference between express and implied contract terms?
- The way in which terms are implied into a contract under common law?
- The operation of statutory implied terms?
- The ways in which exclusion clauses may be incorporated into a contract?
- The common law rules relating to the validity of exclusion clauses?
- The statutory controls placed on the operation of exclusion clauses by the Unfair Contract Terms Act 1977 and the Unfair Terms in Consumer Contract Regulations 1999?
- The elements of misrepresentation?
- The differences between fraudulent, negligent and innocent misrepresentation?
- Remedies that may be available for misrepresentation?
- The operation of common, mutual and unilateral mistake?
- Remedies that may be available for mistake?
- The principles of illegality in contract?
- The nature of duress and the effect that it has on a contract?
- The development of duress from threats of personal violence to threats towards property?
- The evolution of economic duress and the factors that determine its availability?
- The circumstances that amount to undue influence and how this differs from duress?
- The different classes of undue influence and their operation?
- The rule relating to discharge by performance and its exceptions?
- The ways in which a contract may be discharged by agreement between the parties?
- The consequences of breach of contract and the distinction between anticipatory and repudiatory breaches?

▌ The evolution of the doctrine of frustration and the operation of the Law Reform (Frustrated Contracts) Act 1943?

▌ The circumstances in which the availability of damages is limited: causation, remoteness and the duty to mitigate?

▌ The distinction between methods of calculating damages: loss of bargain and reliance loss?

▌ How special categories of damages, such as loss of amenity, mental distress and loss of a chance, are assessed?

▌ The circumstances in which specific performance is available as a remedy for breach of contract?

Glossary of terms

The glossary is divided into two parts: **key definitions** and **other useful terms**. The key definitions can be found within the chapters in which they occur as well as at the end of the book. These definitions are the essential terms that you must know and understand in order to prepare for an exam. The additional list of terms provides further definitions of useful terms and phrases which will also help you answer examination and coursework questions effectively. These terms are highlighted in the text as they occur but the definition can only be found here.

Key definitions

Term	Definition
Acceptance	Final and unqualified expression of assent to the terms of an offer.
Actionable misrepresentation	A statement of material fact made prior to the contract by one party to the contract to the other which is false or misleading and which induced the other party to enter into the contract.
Battle of the forms	The situation that arises where one or both parties attempts to rely on their standard terms is often referred to as the 'battle of the forms'.
Breach of contract	Committed when a party without lawful excuse fails or refuses to perform what is due from them under the contract, or performs defectively or incapacitates themselves from performing.
Damages	A financial remedy that aims to compensate the injured party for the consequences of the breach of contract.
Duty to mitigate	Principle of contract law whereby the innocent party who has suffered a breach of contract has a duty to take reasonable steps to minimise the extent of their loss arising from the breach.

Frustration	Under the doctrine of frustration a contract may be discharged if, after its formation, events occur making its performance impossible or illegal and in certain analogous situations.
Invitation to treat	A preliminary statement expressing a willingness to receive offers.
Mirror image rule	The principle that a valid acceptance must correspond exactly with the terms of the offer is sometimes referred to as the 'mirror image rule'.
Offer	An expression of willingness to contract on specified terms, made with the intention that it is to become binding as soon as it is accepted by the person to whom it is addressed.
Offeree	The party to whom an offer is addressed.
Offeror	The party who makes an offer.
Puff	A boastful statement made in advertising.
Representation	A statement which induces a party to enter into a contract (but does not form part of it).
Revocation	The rescinding, annulling or withdrawal of an offer.
Severable obligations	A contract imposes severable obligations if payment under it is due from time to time as performance of a specified part of the contract is rendered.
Specific performance	An equitable remedy that compels the party in breach to perform his part of the contract.
Term	A promise or undertaking which becomes part of the contract itself.
Unilateral offer	An offer where one party promises to pay the other a sum of money (or to do some other act) if the other will do something (or forbear from doing so) without making any promise to that effect.

Other terms

Term	Definition
Agent	The agent is a party to the contract with the third party. The agent has a direct contractual relationship with the third party, but makes the contract on behalf of the principal and not on his own behalf.
Bilateral contract	A contract in which each party undertakes an obligation.
Common mistake	A category of mistake in which both parties make the same mistake.

Condition	A key term in a contract. If breached, the injured party can repudiate the contract.
Consideration	Consideration is an act or promise of forbearance which 'buys' the promise of the other party. Consideration renders a promise enforceable in law.
Innominate term	Term where the court looks at the effects of the breach on the injured party to determine whether the breach itself was of a condition or a warranty.
Mitigation of loss	A duty to keep one's losses to a minimum.
Mutual mistake	A category of mistake where the parties are at cross-purposes, but each believes that the other is in agreement.
Principal	The party on whose behalf a contract is made and who receives the benefit arising under the contract.
Quantum meruit	'As much as is deserved'. If a price has not been specified in a contract but work has been done or goods supplied under it, a *quantum meruit* action allows a claim for a reasonable price for the performance rendered.
Repudiation	Rejection of the continued existence of a contract.
Uberrimae fidei	'Of utmost good faith'. Essential for the validity of certain contracts between parties with a particular relationship between them, such as contracts of insurance.
Unilateral contract	A contract in which only one party undertakes an obligation.
Unilateral mistake	A category of mistake where one party is mistaken and the other knows and takes advantage of the mistake.
Void contract	A contract which is treated as though it never existed so that it may be enforced by neither party.
Voidable contract	A contract in which the injured party can choose whether or not to be bound by it.
Warranty	A less important term in a contract. If breached, the injured party may sue for damages but is not entitled to repudiate the contract.

Index